Property and Conveyancing Library

LEASEHOLD ENFRANCHISEMENT

AUSTRALIA
Lawbook Co.
Sydney

CANADA AND USA
Carswell
Toronto

HONG KONG
Sweet & Maxwell Asia

NEW ZEALAND
Brookers
Auckland

SINGAPORE AND MALAYSIA
Sweet & Maxwell Asia
Singapore and Kuala Lumpur

PROPERTY AND CONVEYANCING LIBRARY

HAGUE
ON
LEASEHOLD
ENFRANCHISEMENT

Second Supplement to the

Fourth Edition

by

ANTHONY RADEVSKY, LL.B.
of the Inner Temple, Barrister

and

DAMIAN GREENISH, B.A.
Solicitor
Senior Partner, Pemberton Greenish

LONDON
SWEET & MAXWELL
2007

Published in 2007 by
Sweet & Maxwell Ltd of
100 Avenue Road
London
NW3 3PF

www.sweetandmaxwell.thomson.com

Printed by Ashford Colour Press Ltd, Gosport, Hants.
Typeset by Interactive Sciences Limited, Gloucester

No natural forests were destroyed to make this product;
only farmed timber was used and replanted.

A C.I.P. Catalogue record for this book is available from the British Library

ISBN 978–1–818–4703444–1

PREFACE

It is four years since the date at which the law was stated in the Fourth Edition, and a further edition might well have been justified at this stage, given the volume of enfranchisement cases that continue to be reported. However, we have decided to deal with the present need to update Hague by producing a Second Supplement. The main reason for postponing a new edition is that several important cases on points of principle are waiting to be decided in the House of Lords, Court of Appeal and Lands Tribunal. We would not wish a new edition to become out-of-date in an important respect as soon as it was published. However, more than two years have passed since the First Supplement, and we do not feel that a Second one can be delayed.

We would like to welcome Alison Readman as our new indexer.

The law is stated as at October 31, 2007.

Anthony Radevsky
Falcon Chambers
Falcon Court
London
EC4Y 1AA

Damian Greenish
Pemberton Greenish
45 Pont Street
London
SW1X 0BX

HOW TO USE THIS SUPPLEMENT

Cross-referencing

This supplement broadly follows the structure of the main work. Where **chapters** in the mainwork have required updating, they are identified in the supplement by reference to the relevant **paragraph number** in the page margin. Additional referencing beyond paragraph numbering has also been provided within the text where necessary by way of further instructions, *e.g.* "Add to end of second sentence" or by specifying the relevant footnote. In contrast, updates to the **appendices** in the mainwork are identified in the supplement by reference to the relevant **page number(s)** in the page margin.

Omitted chapters

Only chapters and appendices requiring updating are included in this supplement. Readers can be assured that chapters omitted are done so intentionally. Chapters omitted are as follows: chapters 8 and 18.

CONTENTS

Leasehold Reform Act 1967—Chapters 2–19

Collective Enfranchisement—Chapters 20–28

Individual New Leases of Flats—Chapters 29–33

PRECEDENTS

APPENDICES

Statutes

Statutory Instruments

TABLE OF CASES

All references are to paragraph number

TABLE OF STATUTES

All references are to paragraph number

TABLE OF STATUTORY INSTRUMENTS

All references are to paragraph number

CHAPTER 1

INTRODUCTION

1.—BACKGROUND

Commonhold

The commonhold provisions were brought into force on September 27, 2004 (SI **1–11**
2004/1832).

The Arguments—justifications

Management

The right to manage came into force in Wales on March 31, 2004: The Common- **1–15**
hold and Leasehold Reform Act 2002 (Commencement No.2 and Savings)
(Wales) Order 2004 SI 2004/669 (W62), set out at Appendix 2S.

4.—EUROPEAN CONVENTION ON HUMAN RIGHTS

Human Rights Act 1998

The Human Rights Act 1998 was also cited in *7 Strathray Gardens Ltd v* **1–36**
Pointstar Shipping and Finance Ltd [2004] EWCA Civ 1669; [2005] 1 E.G.L.R.
53 but the Court of Appeal did not have to apply it because the case was decided
on other grounds. A petition for leave to appeal to the House of Lords has been
dismissed.

In *Howard de Walden Estates Ltd v Aggio* [2007] 3 W.L.R. 542 in which two
appeals were heard, Arden L.J. (at paras 62–64) expressed reservations about
whether the landlord's rights under Article 1 of the First Protocol to the Convention would have been interefered with, had the court found that a new lease of a
flat could be granted to a head lessee. This was because the 1993 Act would have
failed to set out with any degree of precision important terms of the new lease in
those circumstances. In the event the Court of Appeal decided the case in the
landlord's favour without needing to resolve the human rights arguments. The
House of Lords has granted the tenants in both appeals leave to appeal, and
appeals are pending.

5.—LEASEHOLD REFORM, HOUSING AND URBAN DEVELOPMENT ACT 1993

Collective enfranchisement

1–38 The last sentence (at the top of p. 26) should refer to "not less than one-half" instead of "more than one-half" of the number of flats in the building.

1–46 Following further substantial criticism of the RTE provisions (see, *e.g* Estates Gazette February 21, 2004 at p. 124), it now appears to be acknowledged by the government that as presently drafted they are unworkable. It is unlikely therefore that they will ever be brought into force in their current form. The section fixing the valuation date at the date of the claim notice came into force in England on February 28, 2005: The Commonhold and Leasehold Reform Act 2002 (Commencement No.5 and Saving and Transitional Provision) Order 2004 (SI 2004/3056), set out at Appendix 2W, and in Wales on May 31, 2005: The Commonhold and Leasehold Reform Act 2002 (Commencement No.3 and Saving and Transitional Provision) (Wales) Order 2005 (SI 2005/1353), set out at Appendix 2Y.

6.—CRITICISMS

(6) Right to Enfranchise (RTE) company

1–56 The fourth sentence should begin: "First, there will be even greater . . . "

1–58 There is not much to suggest that matters have improved. See, *e.g.* Solicitors Journal December 5, 2003 at p. 1383.

1–62 **Roll-over relief**

It may well be that relief can be claimed where all the qualifying criteria are satisfied even though the formal statutory procedure is not followed.

CHAPTER 2

ACQUIRING THE FREEHOLD—PREMISES QUALIFYING

1.—HOUSE

Definition

The abolition of a general residence test has led to claims being made in respect **2–02**
of buildings which might not, in the ordinary sense of the word, be considered a
"house". A number of such cases are being pursued and the courts will no doubt
be required to give further guidance on what has become an uncertain area.

"Designed or adapted for living in" **2–04**
In *Boss Holdings Ltd v Grosvenor West End Properties Ltd* [2006] EWCA Civ
594; [2006] 1 W.L.R. 2848, the Court of Appeal considered two cases in which
these words were in issue. In the first, the upper floors of a building originally
constructed as a house, had been used as residential flats and the ground floor as
offices. When a claim to acquire the freehold was made, the former residential
accommodation had become dilapidated and incapable of being used as resi-
dences. In the second case, *Mallett & Son (Antiques) Ltd v Grosvenor West End
Properties Ltd,* the building had also been constructed as a residence but had
been converted for use as an antiques showroom and workshops with an ancillary
caretaker's flat. The tenants' claims were dismissed; Laws L.J. holding (at
paragraph 18) that the true question is whether the premises, or at least a
substantial part, viewed at the moment when the notice is given, were designed
or adapted for living in. Is residence the purpose of the design or adaptation at
the time of the notice? Premises designed or adapted for a different use altogether
might in various sets of circumstances with a little ingenuity be lived in perfectly
readily, but they would not be a house within s. 2(1). The House of Lords granted
the tenants leave to appeal in both cases. In *Mallett & Son (Antiques) Ltd v
Grosvenor West End Properties Ltd,* an appeal was not pursued; in *Boss Holdings
Ltd v Grosvenor West End Properties Ltd,* the appeal is due to be heard in
December 2007.

Boss Holdings was followed in *Colliers CRE Plc v The Portman Estate
Nominees (One) Ltd* (unreported, 2006, Central London County Court). Two
eighteenth-century terraced buildings, built and originally used as houses, had
been fitted out and used as professional offices for many years. Shortly prior to

the claims being made, the lessee carried out unauthorised alterations to make the buildings look more like houses internally. It made good the openings in the party wall, installed bathrooms and a kitchen. H.H. Judge Levy Q.C. held that the claims failed. He found that the tenant should not be allowed to rely on the alterations, as otherwise it would be taking advantage of its own wrong, but even if those works could be taken into account, the statutory test was not satisfied. Permission to appeal was granted but an appeal was not brought.

2–05 *"Reasonably so called"*
In *Hareford Ltd v Barnet London Borough Council* [2005] 2 E.G.L.R. 72, *Tandon* was applied in the case of a purpose-built maisonette above a shop in a parade of similar properties, which was accordingly a house reasonably so called. The tenant did not occupy the shop and so there was no residence test to satisfy under s. 1(1B). The abolition of the residence test by the 2002 Act had the effect of allowing investor lessees to acquire the freehold in those circumstances.

In *Creditforce Ltd v Lay* (unreported, 2007, Central London County Court), it was held by H.H. Judge Levy Q.C. that a building constructed in the nineteenth-century as five flats (since divided into ten flats) above two shops was a house reasonably so called. He granted permission to appeal to the Court of Appeal, and the appeal is due to be heard in January 2008.

Identification of "house"
2–09 Footnotes 68 and 71: *Collins v Howard de Walden Estates Ltd* is also reported at [2003] H.L.R. 70, which is the only report containing the plan of the premises referred to in the judgments.

2.—"HOUSE AND PREMISES"

Meaning of "premises"

"Garden"
2–14 Footnotes 79 and 81: *Methuen-Campbell* is spelt with a "p".

"Appurtenances"
2–16 Footnotes 83, 84 and 86: *Methuen-Campbell* is spelled with a "p".

CHAPTER 3

ACQUIRING THE FREEHOLD—TENANCIES QUALIFYING

1.—LONG TENANCY

Primary definition

Add: *Green v Alexander Johnson* [2004] P.N.L.R. 40 is a cautionary tale of a **3–03** professional negligence action concerning the failure to spot that a claim by a tenant (of a flat under the 1993 Act) holding a lease for a backdated term was not valid, since the tenant did not hold a long tenancy. The decision concerned the correct assessment of damages.

In *Lay v Ackerman (No.2)* (unreported, 2006, Central London County Court) it was held that a claim for a new lease of a flat situated within the house made under the 1993 Act did not prevent the long lease of the house (as opposed to the flat alone) from expiring by effluxion of time. The tenant relied upon Paragraph 5 of Schedule 12 to the 1993 Act, but H.H. Judge Cowell held that that provision applied to the lease only insofar as it demised the flat. *Malekshad v Howard de Walden Estates Ltd No.2* [2004] 1 W.L.R. 862, which held that a notice under the 1967 Act prevented the lease of the whole premises demised by the lease from expiring by effluxion of time under paragraph 3(1) of Schedule 3 to the 1967 Act, was distinguished. Permission to appeal was granted and an appeal to the Court of Appeal is pending, but adjourned until the conclusion of the appeal to the House of Lords in *Howard de Walden Estates Ltd v Aggio* [2007] EWCA Civ 499.

Exception

Under s. 3(1) of the 1967 Act, a lease terminable by a notice after death or **3–05** *et* marriage will be a long tenancy unless it fulfils three conditions. Under s. 1B, if *seq.* that lease was granted before April 18, 1980 then it will only be a long tenancy for the purpose of a freehold claim; *i.e.* it will not be a long tenancy for the purpose of an extended lease claim.

It follows that the right to enfranchise is not in any circumstances "exercisable" by virtue of s. 1B as appears to be anticipated by the draftsman in ss. 1(3A)(b), 9(1C), and 32A(b). The right to enfranchise was extended by s. 64 of the 1993 Act but that arose by virtue of subs. (2) which amended the primary definition of long tenancy in s. 3(1) of the 1967 Act and not by virtue of subs. (1)

which introduced s. 1B [*N.B.* The proviso to s. 3(1) of the 1967 Act was not correctly set out in Appendix 1A of the Fourth Edition. The correct version is set out in Appendix 1A of this Supplement.] What the draftsman seems to have assumed is that the enfranchisement rights were extended by s. 1B. What in fact s. 1B did was restrict enfranchisement rights in consequence of the amendments made to s. 3(1).

The current position seems to be therefore that a long tenancy terminable by notice after death or marriage which does not fulfil the terms of the proviso to s. 3(1) will qualify for both freehold and lease extension claims unless the tenancy was granted before April 18, 1980 in which event it will qualify for a freehold claim only. That was not quite what was intended. What was intended was that the "saving provision" for the "Prince of Wales clause" for tenancies granted before April 18, 1980 should be removed for the purpose of a freehold claim.

This apparent drafting error makes the interpretation of the cross-references to s. 1B in other parts of the Act difficult. In s. 1(3A) it was intended that the right to acquire the freehold from a charitable housing trust of a house which forms part of the housing accommodation provided by the trust in pursuit of its charitable purposes should not be conferred in circumstances where the lease was granted before April 18, 1980 with an effective "Prince of Wales clause". There was a similar intention in respect of qualifying property under s. 32A. The drafting of s. 1B would appear to defeat that intention.

It was also the clear intention that any property that became enfranchisable by virtue of the abolition of the saving for the pre-April 18, 1980 "Prince of Wales clause" should be valued under s. 9(1C). That would also appear to be ineffective because the right to acquire the freehold does not arise "by virtue of" s. 1B but by virtue of the amendments made to the proviso to s. 3(1) of the 1967 Act by s. 64(2) of the 1993 Act. Since the Civil Partnership Act 2004 came into force on December 5, 2005, a tenancy taking effect under s. 149(6) of the Law of Property Act 1925 includes a lease terminable after the formation of a civil partnership.

3–07 Footnote 47: Since the Civil Partnership Act 2004 came into force on December 5, 2005, this includes in addition a termination notice capable of being given at any time after the formation of a civil partnership where the tenancy can be terminated on that basis.

Continuation tenancies

(1) Statutory extensions

3–10 Footnote 71: Where Sch. 10 has effect in relation to a former 1954 Act tenancy the term date of which falls before January 15, 1999, any reference in Sch. 10 to the dwelling-house (or the property) let under the tenancy has effect as a reference to the premises qualifying for protection within the meaning of the 1954 Act. Furthermore, any question of what are the premises qualifying for protection or what is the tenancy shall be determined for the purposes of Sch. 10 in accordance with Pt I of the 1954 Act where Sch. 10 applies to a former 1954

Act tenancy (paragraph 22 of Sch. 10 to the Local Government and Housing Act 1989).

(2) *Renewal tenancies*
The first line should commence: "Certain tenancies granted by way of renewal **3–11** of a previous long tenancy . . .".
    Footnote 82: The appeal in *John Lyon's Charity v Rapp* was not pursued.

Consecutive long tenancies
Footnote 92: The appeal in *John Lyon's Charity v Rapp* was not pursued.   **3–12**

Business tenancies
(c) See paragraph 3–05 above.

Footnote 106: Section 23 of the Landlord and Tenant Act 1954 has been amended   **3–15** by paragraph 13 of the Regulatory Reform (Business Tenancies) (England and Wales) Order 2003 SI 2003/3096.

2.—Low Rent

A. Background

In consequence of the saving provision in paragraph 2(2) of the Schedule to the   **3–17** Housing Act 1996 (Commencement No.10 and Transitional Provisions) Order 1997 SI 1997/6128, the low rent test also remains applicable where the house and premises are held under a tenancy granted by a housing association (whether or not it remains owned by that association) which is a shared ownership lease within the meaning of s. 622 of the Housing Act 1985. In July 2007 the Department for Communities and Local Government issued a Consultation document proposing to remove this saving—see paragraph 14–30, below.

C. The proviso to section 4(1)

"The letting value of the property (on the same terms)"

"Letting value"
Footnote 210: The page reference should be 845F, not 895F.   **3–31**

D. The 1993 Act Test

The alternative low rent test

Tenancies granted between April 1, 1963 and March 31, 1990
In *Neville v Cowdray Trust Ltd* [2006] EWCA Civ 709; [2006] 1 W.L.R. 2097,   **3–47** it was held that it is the rateable value of the "property" demised by the lease that

must be considered under s. 4A(2), not the "house" or the "house and premises". Where two semi-detached cottages were demised, with a lessee's covenant to convert them into a single house, it was the rateable value of the cottages that was taken into account, and not the later rateable value of the newly rated house.

Tenancies granted on or after April 1, 1990

3–49 Footnote 300: In *Cadogan v Strauss* [2004] 2 E.G.L.R. 69, the appeal was dismissed by the Court of Appeal.

Chapter 4

ACQUIRING THE FREEHOLD—PERSONS QUALIFYING

1.—Tenant

Exceptions

(3) See paragraph 3–05 *et seq.*, above.   **4–02**

(4) In *Brick Farm Management Ltd v Richmond Housing Partnership Ltd* [2005] 1 W.L.R. 3934, it was held that, for the purposes of s. 5(2)(b) of the 1993 Act, the housing accommodation provided by a charitable housing trust was restricted to the social housing it provided. That did not include flats let on long leases where the trust had acquired the freehold from a local authority which had granted the long leases under the right to buy provisions of the Housing Act 1985.

It should be noted that it is possible for a charitable housing trust to grant a long lease at a premium: *Joseph Rowntree Memorial Trust Housing Association Ltd v Attorney-General* [1983] Ch. 159.

2.—Qualifying Occupation

Flats

The references to chapter 1 and Chapter/chapter 2 in this paragraph are refer-   **4–04**
ences to the Chapters in Pt 1 of the 1993 Act. The references to Chapters 23 and 29 are to Chapters in this book.

Add to Footnote 47. That which was agreed in the *Crean Davidson* case was decided by the High Court. In *Maurice v Hollow-Ware Products Ltd* [2005] E.W.H.C. 815 (Ch); [2005] 2 E.G.L.R. 71 it was held that the lessee of a block of 28 flats was the qualifying tenant of each flat for the purposes of Chapter 2, and could claim individual new leases of each flat. The landlord's argument that practical conveyancing difficulties would be caused in that event, such that the draftsman could not have intended to include within the definition of qualifying tenant the lessee of a whole building, was rejected. Deputy Judge Donaldson Q.C. held, on the contrary, that ss. 39(4) and 101(3) of the 1993 Act made specific provision for leases where more than a single flat was demised. However, in *Howard de Walden Estates Ltd v Aggio* [2007] EWCA Civ 499; [2007] 3 W.L.R. 542; 3 All E.R. 910, the Court of Appeal (hearing two appeals) overruled *Maurice v Hollow-Ware Products Ltd.* It held that a headlessee whose lease demised not only one or more flats, but also common parts could not be a qualifying tenant. The Act lacked any clear provisions to deal with the terms of a new lease to be granted to such a tenant, which indicated that Parliament had not intended a head lessee to be a qualifyng tenant. In July 2007, the House of Lords granted the tenants in both appeals leave to appeal, and the appeals are pending.

Add the following footnote at the end: In *Cadogan v Search Guarantees Plc* [2004] 1 W.L.R. 2768 [2005]; 1 All E.R. 280 the Court of Appeal held that the head-lessee could not be the qualifying tenant of a flat for the purposes of s. 1(1ZB). The tenant of the flat must be someone other than the tenant of the house.

Business tenancies

4–05   The issue of whether a head landlord who sublets flats in a building holds a business tenancy for the purpose of the 1954 Act was argued before the Court of Appeal in *Cadogan v Search Guarantees Plc* [2004] 1 W.L.R. 2768; [2005] 1 All E.R. 280. However, since the issue had not been raised in the County Court, the Court of Appeal did not consider it.

"As his residence"

4–07   Footnote 61: The court in brackets should read "Central London C.C."

Evidence of occupation

4–11   Footnote 77: Equivalent Regulations came into force in Wales on March 31, 2004. These are set out at Appendix 2V.

3.—SUCCESSION TO TENANCY ON DEATH

4–12   Since the Civil Partnership Act 2004 came into force on December 5, 2005, the reference to "wife or husband" in ss. 7(7) and 7(8) is replaced by "spouse or civil partner".

4.—PERSONAL REPRESENTATIVES

4–13   Under s. 27(1) of the Land Registration Act 2002 a disposition of a registered estate, which is required to be completed by registration, does not operate at law until the relevant registration requirements are met. By virtue of s. 27(5) this applies equally to dispositions by operation of law but under subs. (a) there is an exception for a transfer on death. It follows that the personal representatives do not need to be registered proprietors of the tenancy for the purpose of fulfilling their two-year ownership period.

CHAPTER 5

STATUTORY NOTICES AND THEIR EFFECT

1.—NOTICE OF TENANT'S CLAIM

Requirements of notice

Particulars required by the prescribed form

Footnote 39: In *Cadogan v Strauss* [2004] 2 E.G.L.R. 69, the appeal was **5–04** dismissed. It was held by the Court of Appeal that the failure by the tenant to refer to the earlier lease, of which he was unaware at the time of giving the notice, was an inaccuracy in the particulars and saved by paragraph 6(3) of Schedule 3 to the 1967 Act.

Validity of the notice

Footnote 64: A view broadly endorsed by Chadwick L.J. in *Cadogan v Strauss* **5–05** [2004] 2 E.G.L.R. 69 when he said at para. [43]: "The purpose—and if I may say so, the obvious purpose—of the particulars set out in paragraph 6(1) of Schedule 3 to the 1967 Act is to enable the landlord to decide whether or not to admit the claim."

Footnote 67: In *Cadogan v Strauss* [2004] 2 E.G.L.R. 69, the Court of Appeal held that the failure by a tenant to refer to an earlier lease (of which he was unaware) which formed a single tenancy by virtue of s.3(3) of the 1967 Act, was an inaccuracy saved by paragraph 6(3) of Schedule 3 to the Act. It considered both *Cresswell* and *Speedwell* ("The common thread in those decisions is that, whether or not a defect in the Leasehold Reform Act notice is to be regarded as an inaccuracy, is essentially a matter to be decided on the facts of each case"—*per* Chadwick L.J. at para. [41]).

Footnote 70: A view not endorsed by the Court of Appeal in *Cadogan v Strauss* [2004] 2 E.G.L.R. 69, where the landlord's knowledge of the earlier leases not referred to the desire notice meant that the landlord could not assert prejudice: Chadwick L.J. at para. [48].

Footnote 72: In *Cadogan v Strauss* [2004] 2 E.G.L.R. 69, the court contrasted the failure to provide any information at all with the failure to provide accurate information: Chadwick L.J. at para. [47].

Footnote 80: The appeal on this point was successful: *Malekshad v Howard de Walden Estates Ltd (No.2)* [2004] 1 W.L.R. 862. If a notice of claim extends to property not properly included in the house and premises or does not extend to property that ought to be so included, it will be invalid if it is not amended. Amending a notice is not simply an "administrative act". However, unless there is dishonesty or similar on the part of the tenant, the court should normally permit an amendment. Furthermore, that amendment should usually be without conditions unless the landlord can establish prejudice in consequence of the amendment. In his judgment, Neuberger J. gave further guidance as to the factors to be taken into account in deciding whether or not a notice should be amended and if so on what terms although he stressed that each case would turn on its own facts.

In *Oakwood Court (Holland Park) Ltd v Daejan Properties Ltd* [2007] 1 E.G.L.R. 121, the equivalent provisions under the 1993 Act were considered. It was held in a collective enfranchisement case that Schedule 3, paragraph 15(2) cannot be read purposively to permit amendments in cases other than those specified. It applies only where the initial notice either specifies property or an interest that the claimant is not entitled to acquire under ss. 1 or 2 of the 1993 Act or fails to specify property or an interest that the claimant is entitled to acquire.

Footnote 82: In *Malekshad v Howard de Walden Estates Ltd (No.2)* [2004] 1 W.L.R. 862, Neuberger J. confirmed the jurisdiction of the court under paragraph 6(3) to move the valuation date although he declined to do so in the particular circumstances of that case.

Add at end of paragraph: It is considered that the decision in *Cadogan v Strauss* [2004] 2 E.G.L.R. 69 has made it difficult for practitioners to advise with confidence whether a particular defect is fatal to a notice or a forgivable inaccuracy. For example, in some cases the knowledge of the landlord is treated as irrelevant; in others, it may be relied on by the tenant to save his notice. The statement referred in Footnote 67 above that cases are to be decided on their own facts, whilst to some extent understandable, is unhelpful in failing to lay down clear principles to be applied in other cases.

Time for service of notice

5–08   (iii) Paragraph 2(1) of Schedule 3 to the 1967 Act has now been replaced by new provisions set out in paragraphs 10/11 of Schedule 5 to the Regulatory Reform (Business Tenancies) (England and Wales) Order 2003 (SI 2003/3096) which came into force on June 1, 2004. The only practical change is that, in place of a stated two-month period, which applied in all cases, the period is now "the relevant time". That is defined to be the end of the period of two months beginning with the date on which the landlord's notice terminating the tenancy is given or (in a case where the tenancy is determined by notice under s. 25 of the 1954 Act), the date of the tenant's application to the court under s. 24(1) of the 1954 Act for the grant of a new tenancy, if that application is made before the expiration of that two month period.

Footnote 117: Now paragraph 2(1D) of Schedule 3.
Footnote 119: Now paragraph 2(1E) of Schedule 3.

Formation of contract

Footnote 143: The relevant procedure is set out in paragraph 5.2 of the Land **5–09**
Registry Practice Guide 27 (November 2006).

2.—Effect of Service of Tenant's Notice

Assignment of benefit

Footnote 149: The reference to the *Melbury Rd* case is [1999] not [1993]. **5–10**

Footnote 154: The reference to Ruoff & Roper is now to paragraph 26.004.
Also, see paragraph 4–13, above. The exceptions in s. 27(5) also extend to
bankruptcy of an individual proprietor—subs. (a)—and dissolution of a corporate
proprietor—subs. (b). In *Typeteam Ltd v Acton* (unreported, 2006, Central London County Court) it was held that an assignment of the benefit of a section 42
notice under the 1993 Act dated the same day as a Transfer of the lease in Form
TR1 was effective, even though the Transfer had yet to be registered at HM Land
Registry. H.H. Judge Cowell held that it was permissible to read s. 43(3) as
referring to the assignment or subsistence of interests either in law or in equity.
The High Court has granted the landlord permission to appeal, and an appeal is
due to be heard in November 2007.

Continuation of tenancy

Footnote 168: It was decided by Neuberger J. in *Malekshad v Howard de Walden* **5–13**
Estates Ltd (No.2) [2004] 1 W.L.R. 862 that the effect of paragraph 3(1) of
Schedule 3 to the 1967 Act is to continue the tenancy, not just in relation to the
property which is the subject of the claim, but in respect of the entirety of the
property comprised in the tenancy.

Footnote 182: This point was also considered by Neuberger J. in *Malekshad v
Howard de Walden Estates Ltd (No.2)* [2004] 1 W.L.R. 862. Acknowledging that
the point was a difficult one, he nevertheless held that the obiter dictum of
Eveleigh L.J. in *Duke of Westminster v Oddy* [1984] 1 E.G.L.R. was wrong and
that:

(i) a tenancy continuing by virtue of paragraph 3(1) remains a long
tenancy; and

(ii) a tenant is entitled to serve a Notice of Tenant's Claim during the
continuation tenancy.

Footnote 184: Now paragraph 2(1B).

Effect on Landlord and Tenant Act 1954 and Local Government and Housing Act 1989 notices

Footnote 186: Now paragraphs 2(1B) and 2(1C). **5–14**

A new paragraph 2A of Schedule 3 to the 1967 Act (added by paragraph 12
of Schedule 5 to the Regulatory Reform (Business Tenancies) (England and
Wales) Order 2003 SI 2003/3096) provides that if:

(i) the landlord commences proceedings under Pt 2 of the 1954 Act; and

(ii) the tenant subsequently makes a claim to acquire the freehold or an extended lease of the property; and

(iii) paragraph 2 of Sch. 3 to the 1967 Act does not invalidate that claim;

then no further steps can be taken in the 1954 Act proceedings otherwise than for their dismissal and for the making of any consequential order.

Footnote 188: It is now provided that s. 64 of the 1954 Act (the interim continuation of a 1954 Act tenancy pending a determination by the court) does not have effect in a case to which paragraph 2A of Schedule 3 to the 1967 Act applies: paragraph 2A(2) of Schedule 3 to the 1967 Act, added by paragraph 12 of Schedule 5 to the Regulatory Reform (Business Tenancies) (England and Wales) Order 2003 SI 2003/3096.

Footnote 198: A new paragraph 10(2A) has been added (by paragraph 13 of Schedule 5 to the Regulatory Reform (Business Tenancies) (England and Wales) Order 2003 SI 2003/3096) so that, in the case of a notice given under s. 25 of the 1954 Act, additional words must be included in the notice to reflect the provisions of paragraph 2A of Schedule 3 to the 1967 Act. The wording has not incidentally been amended to reflect the new paragraphs 2(1), *et seq.*

3.—Obligations of Recipient of Tenant's Notice

Landlord's Notice in Reply

5–19 It was argued in *Earl Cadogan v Search Guarantees Plc* [2005] 1 All E.R. 280; [2004] 1 W.L.R. 2768, that there was no absolute right for a landlord to be able to rely on grounds of opposition to a claim which were not contained in his Notice in Reply. However, the Court of Appeal declined to consider in what circumstances and subject to what limitations a landlord might be entitled to do so: *per* Laddie J. at paragraphs [20]–[24].

If a tenant suffers damage in consequence of a landlord's failure to serve a Notice in Reply (or in consequence of service of an invalid or incomplete one) then the tenant might well have a claim against the landlord, either in negligence or for breach of statutory duty: see *7 Strathray Gardens Ltd v Pointstar Shipping and Finance Ltd* [2004] EWCA Civ 1669; [2005] 1 E.G.L.R. 53, *per* Arden L.J. at para. [54], Jacob L.J. at para. [56] and Ward L.J. at para. [57]. That case was concerned with a counter-notice given under s. 21 of the 1993 Act.

On p. 129, the suggestion that the Notice in Reply must in all cases state the matters set out in paragraphs (a) and (b) is not correct; those matters are only required to be stated in those cases where the landlord admits the claim.

CHAPTER 6

ACQUIRING THE FREEHOLD—ACQUISITION TERMS

1.—CONDITIONS OF STATUTORY CONTRACT

Footnote 7: Equivalent Regulations were brought into force in Wales on March **6–02**
31, 2004.

2.—ESTATE TO BE CONVEYED

"Incumbrances" and "tenant's incumbrances"
Line 2—should read "to tenant's incumbrances" not "the".   **6–12**

3.—CONTENTS OF CONVEYANCE

Specific rights
Footnote 109: now paragraph 5.1 of Land Registry Practice Guide 27 (November **6–18**
2006).
   Footnote 110: now paragraph 5.3.1 of Land Registry Practice Guide 27
(November 2006).

Rights of Way
In *Kent v Kavanagh* [2006] EWCA Civ 162; [2007] Ch. 1, the Court of Appeal **6–19**
considered what right of way had been conveyed over a shared pathway between
two houses, each of which had been enfranchised from the same landlord under
the 1967 Act. It was held (1) that the first rule in *Wheeldon v Burrows* (1879) 12
Ch D 31 could have no application where, at the time of the conveyance, the land
conveyed and the land retained, although in common ownership, were not in
common occupation; that, therefore, the rule had no application to a conveyance
executed to give effect to a landlord's obligation to enfranchise imposed by
s. 8(1) of the 1967 Act. However, where one part of a piece of land in common
ownership was occupied by a tenant and was conveyed to the tenant under the
1967 Act, s. 62 of the Law of Property Act 1925 was apt to convey, with the
freehold, rights of way over the freehold of the retained land which were, at the

time of the conveyance, enjoyed by the tenant in occupation of the land conveyed. It was proper to construe a conveyance executed to give effect to s. 8(1)
of the 1967 Act as being subject to the tenancy and to tenant's incumbrances,
whether or not it contained express words of reservation, since that was the
extent of the obligation imposed on the landlord by s. 8(1) and the parties were
to be taken to have intended that the conveyance would give effect to that
obligation. A right in the nature of an easement, reserved out of the leasehold
interest at the time when the tenancy was granted, was a "tenant's incumbrance"
for the purposes of s. 8(1). Therefore, such a right would be reserved out of the
freehold of the conveyed land for the benefit of the retained land. It was also held,
(2) where the conveyed land and the retained land had both been held under
tenancies from a common owner and the tenant of each plot had had reciprocal
rights over the leasehold interest in the other plot, the former tenant of the
conveyed plot would continue to enjoy the rights over the leasehold interest of
the retained plot which he had enjoyed as tenant, and the tenant of the retained
plot would continue to enjoy the rights over the conveyed plot to which he was
entitled under his lease, since those rights would be tenant's incumbrances to
which the freehold of the conveyed plot would be subject. It was also held, (3)
if the retained land were subsequently enfranchised, s. 62 of the 1925 Act
operated to convey with the freehold the rights over the freehold of the originally
conveyed land which had been reserved to the former common owner on the
original conveyance. After enfranchisement of both plots the former tenants
continued to enjoy the same rights over each other's plots as they did while they
were tenants.

Easements and rights to be reserved

Specific rights

6–22   Footnote 127: now paragraph 5.1 of Land Registry Practice Guide 27 (November
2006).

Footnote 128: now paragraph 5.3.1 of Land Registry Practice Guide 27
(November 2006).

Restrictive covenants

Generally

6–26   Footnote 143: The appeal in *Moreau* was not pursued.

Restrictive covenants in tenant's lease

6–28   Footnote 152: The appeal in *Moreau* was not pursued. These cases were applied
by the Lands Tribunal in *Higgs v Nieroba* (unreported, 2005), where restrictions
on carrying out alterations without consent were included in the transfer, even
though only one property benefitted from them.

New restrictive covenants

6–30   Footnote 156: The appeal in *Moreau* was not pursued.

4.—MERGER

The requirements of the Land Registry are now set out in Appendix 1 to Land   **6–36**
Registry Practice Guide 27 (November 2006).

5.—WITHDRAWAL AND COSTS OF ENFRANCHISEMENT

Other costs

(a) the landlord's valuation costs. In *Blendcrown Ltd v Church Commis-*   **6–39**
sioners for England [2004] 1 E.G.L.R. 143, the Lands Tribunal (in
assessing costs recoverable under s. 33 of the 1993 Act) held that a
reasonable valuation fee should have been based on an hourly rate as
opposed to a scale fee on value.

Footnote 201 should begin: "This would include costs that consist of foregoing an advantage that the landlord would otherwise have had: *Re Cressingham
Properties Ltd* [1999] 2 E.G.L.R. 117, P.H. Clarke FRICS citing . . ."

Chapter 7

EXTENDING THE LEASE

3.—Tenancies Qualifying

Tenancies terminable on death or marriage
See paragraph 3–05 *et seq.*, above.   **7–25**

6.—Conditions of Statutory Contract

Preliminary
Footnote 119: Equivalent Regulations were brought into force in Wales on March   **7–29**
31, 2004. They are set out in Appendix 2V.

9.—Registration of Title

The requirements of the Land Registry are now set out in Appendix 2 to Land   **7–45**
Registry Practice Guide 27 (November 2006).

11.—Miscellaneous

Tenant's estate subject to mortgage

Generally
Footnote 193: Now Appendix 2 to Land Registry Practice Guide 27 (November   **7–50**
2006); it seems that the Land Registry still does not accept this proposition.

Registered land
The relevant procedure is now set out in Appendix 2 to Land Registry Practice   **7–51**
Guide 27 (November 2006).

CHAPTER 9

ACQUIRING THE FREEHOLD—VALUATION

1.—VALUATION UNDER SECTION 9(1)

Qualification

Footnote 4: See paragraph 3–05 *et seq.*, above.   **9–02**

(1) Capitalised value of the rent payable for the period of the unexpired term of the existing tenancy

Footnote 56: See also *Blendcrown Ltd v Church Commissioners for England*   **9–09**
[2004] 1 E.G.L.R. 143 *per* P.H. Clarke F.R.I.C.S at para. 53. See also *Arbib v
Earl Cadogan* [2005] 3 E.G. 139, para. [180] (4).

Footnote 58: See also *The Trustees of the Simon J Day Settlement* (LRA/
28/2003, Lands Tribunal, unreported) *per* P.R. Francis at para. 21: "Consideration of trends in the money markets generally is valid . . . Obviously, money
market trends alone are insufficient to form a proper conclusion, and there can be
no substitute for hard evidence."

The rate used to capitalise the freeholder's rental income should usually be
considered separately from the deferment rate: *Nicholson v Goff* [2007] 1
E.G.L.R. 83, where at para. 9 the Lands Tribunal listed the factors which would
influence that rate. These were: (i) the length of the lease term, (ii) the security
of recovery, (iii) the size of the ground rent (a larger ground rent being more
attractive), (iv) whether there was provision for review of the ground rent, and (v)
if there were such provision, the nature of it. This case was concerned with a
valuation under Schedule 13 to the 1993 Act but it is considered that the same
factors would apply to a valuation under section 9 of the 1967 Act.

Settlement Evidence

In *Arbib v Earl Cadogan* [2005] 3 E.G.L.R. 139, para. [180] (7), the Lands
Tribunal held that settlements relating to comparable properties are admissable as
evidence of value, but are subject to criticism and will usually be given weight
only where a detailed analysis of the price or value has been agreed and the
agreement has not been influenced by the *Delaforce* effect.

Value of the landlord's ultimate reversion

The Haresign addition

9–12 In *Re Khan* (unreported, 2004, LVT) and some other cases, it was held that the effect of s. 143 of the Commonhold and Leasehold Reform Act 2002 was to preclude the inclusion of the Haresign addition, because a tenant who has extended his lease is now entitled to acquire the freehold. That decision is wholly misconceived. It overlooks the fact that s. 9(1)(a) of the Act, which requires the assumption to be made in the valuation that the tenant does not have the right to acquire the freehold, remains unaffected by s. 143 of the 2002 Act.

2.—VALUATION OF FREEHOLD UNDER SECTION 9(1A)

Valuation assumptions

(a) *Estate sold*

9–26 If the relevant date (*i.e.* the date that the Notice of Tenant's Claim is given) is on or before the original term date, then the assumptions apply as if the tenancy terminates on the original term date: s. 9(1AA)(a) inserted by s. 143(4) of the 2002 Act.

(d) *Improvements*

9–30— In *Fattal v Keepers and Governors of the Free Grammar School of John Lyon*
9–31 [2004] EWCA Civ 1530; [2005] 1 W.L.R. 803, the Court of Appeal upheld the Lands Tribunal (P. Francis FRICS) on two points. Firstly, development potential, including in particular the value of any planning permission obtained by the tenant, should not be disregarded in valuing the property. Secondly, s. 9(1A)(d) does not impose any methodology as to how the assumption is given effect in valuation terms. The method is a matter of valuation, not law. The proposition stated in the Fourth Edition at p. 225, namely:

> "The manner in which the assumption is given effect is for the property to be valued (at all stages of the valuation—including the calculation of the marriage value) as if the improvements had not been made"

was cited with approval at para. 18 of Sir Martin Nourse's judgment. The House of Lords has dismissed a petition for leave to appeal.

In *Eyre Estate v Alliance* (unreported, 2004) the leasehold valuation tribunal (Chairman: Professor J. Farrand Q.C.) followed the second paragraph of the text in holding that the demolition of one house and its replacement by another was a tenant's improvement. The tribunal rejected the landlord's argument that the provision of the house which existed at the valuation date could not be an improvement by reason of the Court of Appeal's decision in *Rosen*.

Footnote 180: The appeal in *Moreau* was not pursued.

Footnote 184: The appeal in *John Lyon's Charity v Rapp* was not pursued.

Purchase price—generally

In some recent cases, landlord's valuers have been seeking to argue that there is   **9–34**
a further element to be included in the valuation, namely "hope value". This was
described in *Earl Cadogan v Sportelli* [2007] 1 E.G. 153 at para. 98 as being the
value of the option that the freeholder has to sell the freehold or a lease extension
to the tenant and thus realise the whole or part of the freeholder's share of such
marriage value as exists at the date of sale. It was decided in that case that "hope
value" could form part of a valuation under s. 9(1A) but in *Pitts & Wang v
Cadogan* [2007] 42 E.G. 246 the tribunal took a contrary view. The Court of
Appeal's decision in *Cadogan v Sportelli* [2007] EWCA Civ 1042, in holding
that hope value was not to be included in valuations under the 1993 Act, also
indicated that *Pitts & Wang* was correct, and that hope value is not payable under
the 1967 Act: Carnwath L.J. at paras 58–59. A petition for leave to appeal to the
House of Lords is expected.

In *Duke of Westminster v Regis Group (Barclays) Ltd* [2007] 38 E.G. 204, the
Lands Tribunal held that there is no presumption that the seller has knowledge of
any special purchaser or the nature of their special interest. It was a matter of
factual evidence whether the seller on the open market would have been aware
of a special purchaser or the nature of his interest.

**(2) Value of landlord's reversion after the original term date, on the
assumptions as to Part I of the Landlord and Tenant Act 1954 and
Schedule 10 to the Local Government and Housing Act 1989 and as to
repairs and improvements mentioned above**

(b) *Deferment Rate*

In *Cadogan Holdings Limited v Pockney* [2005] R.V.R. 197, the landlord per-   **9–37**
suaded the Lands Tribunal (N.J. Rose FRICS) to depart from what had become
the accepted convention of a deferment rate of six per cent for prime central
London property broadly derived from settlement evidence and determined a rate
of 5.25 per cent. See also *The Trustees of the Simon J Day Settlement* (LRA/
28/2003, Lands Tribunal, unreported). However, this departure from the settlement evidence was not subsequently adopted by the leasehold valuation tribunal.
Two further rafts of appeals went to the Lands Tribunal; *Arbib v Earl Cadogan*
[2005] 3 E.G.L.R. 139, and *Earl Cadogan v Sportelli* [2007] 1 E.G.L.R. 153. In
Sportelli at para. 52, the Lands Tribunal defined the deferment rate as the annual
discount applied, on a compound basis, to an anticipated future receipt (assessed
at current prices) to arrive at its market value at the valuation date. The eventual
outcome has been to promote a standard deferment rate applicable to all properties across the country of 4.75 per cent for houses and five per cent for flats. This
resulted from a detailed consideration of financial evidence, the view being taken
that property market evidence was tainted by statutory enfranchisement rights.
The rate was obtained by taking a risk premium of 4.5 per cent, in combination
with a risk free rate of 2.25 per cent and a real growth rate of 2 per cent (which
is deducted) producing a generic deferment rate of 4.75 per cent. The imposition
of a standard rate to apply regardless of location has proved controversial. The
Court of Appeal has dismissed the appeals against the Lands Tribunal's decision

on deferment rate: [2007] EWCA Civ 1042. It adopted the same definition of deferment rate (para. 3). This is effectively binding guidance for properties within the Prime Central London area. Outside that area, it remains open to valuers to seek to argue for a different rate, using 4.75 per cent as the starting point: *per* Carnwath L.J. at para. 102.

In *Arbib* the Lands Tribunal indicated that, once a deferment rate has been established, it should be generally applied until evidence of a change in the risk free rate justified a "step gradation"; short term fluctuations in interest rates should not lead to changes in the established deferment rate. In *Sportelli* the Lands Tribunal added at para. 122 that the deferment rate may be treated as being stable over time unless a trend movement in the risk-free rate can be identified or it can be established that the long term prospects of growth in residential property have changed or that, for some other reason, the attraction of investment in residential reversions can be shown to have increased or diminished.

9–40   (a) *Calculation of marriage value*
In *Pitts & Wang v Cadogan* [2007] 42 E.G. 296, the Lands Tribunal held, contrary to its earlier decision in *Earl Cadogan v Sportelli* [2007] 1 E.G.L.R. 153, that the fact that marriage value was payable by the tenant precluded the inclusion of "hope value" in the valuation of the landlord's reversion. In this context, "hope value" means the prospect of the landlord being able to grant the tenant a new lease before the contractual expiry date of the current lease. The Court of Appeal's decision in *Cadogan v Sportelli* [2007] EWCA Civ 1042, in holding that hope value was not to be included in valuations under the 1993 Act, also indicated that *Pitts & Wang* was correct, and that hope value is not payable under the 1967 Act: Carnwath L.J. at paras 58–59. A petition for leave to appeal to the House of Lords is expected.

In *Arrowdell Ltd v Coniston Court (North) Hove Ltd* [2007] R.V.R. 39, the Lands Tribunal held that settlements and tribunal decisions were unreliable as evidence of the correct relativity of leases to freeholds. At para. 57 it considered that graphs of relativity published by firms of valuers are capable of providing the most useful guidance and expressed the hope that the RICS would be able to produce a standard graph. It is understood that a RICS working party has been formed to look at this.

4.—VALUATION UNDER SECTION 9(1C)

Basis of valuation

Notice given after the original term date
9–52   The modifications are set out in s. 9(1AA)(b) of the 1967 Act inserted by s. 143(4) of the 2002 Act.

CHAPTER 10

LANDLORD'S OVERRIDING RIGHTS

2.—RESIDENTIAL RIGHTS

Grounds of application

Since the Civil Partnership Act 2004 came into force on December 5, 2005, the   **10–08**
reference to "wife or husband" in s. 18(3) has been replaced by "spouse or civil
partner".

CHAPTER 11

SUB-TENANTS

3.—EXTENDED LEASE

Onerous or valueless intermediate tenancy
In the fourth line from the bottom of p. 264 the word "reversion" should read   **11–21**
"revision".

CHAPTER 12

RENTCHARGES

Now paragraph 5.3.3 of the Land Registry Practice Guide 27 (November **12–01** 2006).

CHAPTER 13

MORTGAGES

1.—ACQUISITION OF FREEHOLD—MORTGAGE OF LANDLORD'S INTEREST

Registered land
Now paragraph 5.3.2 of Land Registry Practice Guide 27 (November 2006).   **13–05**

CHAPTER 14

SPECIAL CLASSES OF LANDLORD

1.—PUBLIC BODIES

Right of possession

Public bodies qualifying
(5) was repealed by the Serious Organised Crime and Police Act 2005, ss. 59, **14–02**
174, Schedule 4, paragraph 17 and Schedule 17 Part 2.
   (7) add Strategic Health Authority and NHS Foundation Trust.

Ministers Certificate
(iv) should now read: in the case of any Strategic Health Authority, Health **14–03**
Authority, any Special Health Authority, any Primary Care Trust, any National
Health Service trust and any NHS foundation trust the purposes of the National
Health Services are substituted for the purposes of that body

Shared ownership leases—generally
See paragraph 14–30, below.   **14–06**

Reservation of development rights
In consequence of s. 177(2) of the Education and Inspections Act 2006, it is no **14–17**
longer necessary for the consent of the Secretary of State for Education to be
obtained for the imposition by a "university body" of covenants under section
29. By s. 177(3) of the Act the possible development for which land may be
reserved by a s. 29 covenant must now be development for the purposes (other
than investment purposes) of the university body or any related university
body.

7.—HOUSING ASSOCIATIONS

Shared ownership leases—generally
In consequence of the saving provision in paragraph 2(2) of the Schedule to the **14–30**
Housing Act 1996 (Commencement No.10 and Transitional Provisions) Order

1997 SI 1997/6128, the low rent test remains applicable where the house and premises are held under a tenancy granted by a housing association (whether or not it remains owned by that association) which is a shared ownership lease within the meaning of s. 622 of the Housing Act 1985.

In July 2007, the Department for Communities and Local Government issued a Consultation document proposing to: (a) allow limits on the further equity shares which shared owners can purchase in specified areas designated by the Secretary of State (where limited land is available for the replacement of affordable housing) without the risk of enfranchisement, (b) allow all providers the opportunity to offer shared ownership leases for houses without the risk of a shared owner enfranchising early to avoid purchasing additional shares through their shared ownership lease, and (c) removing the saving provision for the low rent test from tenancies granted after the relevant legislation comes into force, as a condition for determining eligibility for enfranchisement.

10.—THE CROWN

14–46 During the passage of the 2002 Act through Parliament, the Parliamentary Secretary, Lord Chancellor's Department (Baroness Scotland of Asthal) stated in a Written Reply:

> "Following a statement made on 2 November 1992 by Sir George Young, the Crown authorities gave an undertaking that the Crown would, as landlord and subject to specified conditions, agree to the enfranchisement or extension of residential long leases under the same qualifications and terms which applied by virtue of the Leasehold Reform Act 1967 and the Leasehold Reform, Housing and Urban Development Act 1993 to lessees who hold from other landlords.
>
> It was announced on 3 April 2001, Official Report, cols, WA 110–112 that the Crown authorities had confirmed that they would apply the undertaking to the provisions of the 1967 Act and the 1993 Act as amended by the Commonhold and Leasehold Reform Bill which was then before Parliament. As was announced by my noble and learned friend Lord Falconer of Thoroton during Third Reading of the Commonhold and Leasehold Reform Bill, which is before this Parliament, on 19 November 2001, (Official Report, col. 927), the Crown authorities have now confirmed that this also applies to those Acts as amended by the current Bill. This undertaking accordingly supersedes the one given on 3 April 2001.
>
> The full terms of the agreement made by the Crown are as follows:
>
> > (1) the Crown as landlord will, subject to the conditions described below, agree to the enfranchisement or extension of residential long leases or the grant of new residential long leases, under the same qualifications and terms which will apply by virtue of the Leasehold Reform Act 1967 and the Leasehold Reform, Housing and Urban Development Act 1993 to lessees who hold from other landlords;

(2) enfranchisement will be refused where property stands on land which is held inalienably;

(3) enfranchisement will also be refused where certain circumstances, which only apply to the Crown, obtain. These are:

    (i) where there are particular security considerations (on the advice of the Royal and Diplomatic Protection Group of the Metropolitan Police or other security agencies);

    (ii) where properties are in, or intimately connected with. the curtilage of historic Royal Parks and Palaces;

    (iii) where properties, or the areas in which they are situated, have a long historic or particular association with the Crown.

(4) the areas referred to in paragraph (3)(iii) include the Off Islands within the Isles of Scilly (St Agnes, Bryher, St Martins and Tresco), the Garrison on St Mary's, the village of Newton St Loe and parts of central Dartmoor. The properties referred to in that paragraph include old land revenue and reverter properties and grace and favour properties;

(5) where enfranchisement is refused on the grounds set out in paragraphs (2) and (3) but the tenant would otherwise qualify for enfranchisement, lease extension or the grant of a new lease by analogy with the statutes, the Crown will be prepared to negotiate new leases;

(6) the Crown will follow the valuation bases set out in the Leasehold Reform Act 1967 and the Leasehold Reform, Housing and Urban Development Act 1993;

(7) the Crown will agree to be bound by arbitration where there is dispute over valuation or other terms, except in cases under paragraphs (2) and (3). The Leasehold Valuation Tribunal will be empowered to act as the arbitration body, and will hear such disputes on voluntary reference;

(8) the Crown will be entitled to apply to the Leasehold Valuation Tribunal for approval of a scheme of estate management in the same way as other landlords."

Jurisdiction for the Leasehold Valuation Tribunal to act as an arbitration body for the purpose of paragraph (7) of the undertaking is conferred by s. 88 of the 1993 Act.

12.—BODIES HOLDING LAND WHICH IS INALIENABLE BY STATUTE

In *Blacker v Wimbledon and Putney Commons Conservators* [2004] 3 E.G.L.R.   **14–48** 67, Judge Williams held that the tenant of a house on Wimbledon Common was entitled to acquire the freehold, notwithstanding that s. 35 of the Wimbledon and Putney Commons Act 1871 made the freehold inalienable. It was held that the private 1871 Act only applied to voluntary disposals by the Conservators, and that the 1967 Act both permitted and obliged them to sell the tenant the freehold. The authorities referred to in this paragraph were held not to apply in this situation, contrary to the view expressed here.

CHAPTER 15

SETTLEMENTS AND TRUSTS

1.—AFFECTING LANDLORD'S INTEREST

Rights under the 1967 Act

Since the Civil Partnership Act 2004 came into force on December 5, 2005, the **15–04** reference to "wife or husband" in s. 18(3) have been replaced by "spouse or civil partner".

Chapter 16

COURT AND TRIBUNAL PROCEEDINGS

1.—High Court

Footnote 7: The commencement date for Wales is March 31, 2004. The Order is **16–01** at Appendix 2S.

3.—Leasehold Valuation Tribunals

Procedure

Certain amendments to the 2003 Regulations have been made, in England only, **16–09** by the Leasehold Valuation Tribunals (Procedure)(Amendment)(England) Regulations 2004. These are set out in Appendix 2X of this Supplement, and apply to applications to the tribunal made on or after February 28, 2005. They include amendments to the provisions regarding determinations without a hearing, and inspection of premises, and require a copy of the lease to be submitted with the application.

Footnote 76: Equivalent Regulations came into force in Wales on March 31, 2004. They are set out at Appendix 2U.

In *De Campomar v Trustees of the Pettiward Estate* [2005] 1 E.G.L.R. 83, the Lands Tribunal allowed the appeal of two tenants, whose applications to the LVT for the terms of new leases to be determined were dismissed as an abuse of process. The LVT had adjourned the applications for six months, having been informed by the parties that the premiums had been agreed and negotiations were continuing in respect of the remaining terms. The applicants forgot to tell the LVT that negotiations were still proceeding when the six months were up, and the LVT dismissed the applications without further notice. Judge Rich Q.C. held (1) that the Lands Tribunal had jurisdiction to hear the appeal under Schedule 22 to the Housing Act 1980, even though the appellants had not appeared at a hearing before the LVT; (2) the LVT had jurisdiction in a proper case to dismiss applications to enforce its rules of practice; but (3) it should not have done so without considering whether there might be grounds for relief from the proposed sanction. In these circumstances, dismissal of the applications would lead to the serious consequences that the s. 42 notices would be rendered ineffective, although neither withdrawn nor deemed withdrawn. Since the sanction imposed was a departure from the requirements of justice, and disproportionate, the appeals were allowed and the applications remitted to the LVT.

Costs

16–10 Also introduced to Wales with effect from March 30, 2004. The Order is at Appendix 2S.

4.—Lands Tribunal

Appeal from leasehold valuation tribunal

16–11 Footnote 108: The commencement date for Wales is March 31, 2004. The Order is at Appendix 25.

Footnote 110: See now the Lands Tribunal (Amendment) Rules 2003, which has made the amendment. The amended Rules are set out in Appendix 2E.

The 2001 Lands Tribunal Practice Direction referred to in the first sentence was replaced by one dated January 4, 2005, which was set out in Appendix 2I of the First Supplement. This in turn was replaced by one dated 11 May 2006, which is set out in Appendix 2I of this Supplement. Of particular significance is Section 5 giving guidance as to the Lands Tribunal's approach to an application for permission to appeal.

In *Arrowdell Ltd v Coniston Court (North) Hove Ltd* [2007] R.V.R. 39 at para. 16 the Lands Tribunal criticised the lack of opportunity for a respondent to cross appeal and expressed the hope that the Rules might be amended to cure this "injustice". No such amendment has to date been forthcoming.

Procedure

16–12 Add to footnote 133: However, in *Arrowdell Ltd v Coniston Court (North) Hove Ltd* [2007] R.V.R. 39, the Lands Tribunal held that there is jurisdiction on appeal to determine, in favour of a respondent a price higher or lower (as the case may be) than that decided on by the LVT, even though the respondent has not cross-appealed. None of the cases referred to in Footnotes 130–133 were cited to the Lands Tribunal. However, see also *Chelsea Properties Limited v Earl Cadogan and Cadogan Estates Ltd* [2007] P.L.S.C.S. 197 where the Lands Tribunal held (paras 15–17) that the respondents could argue for a figure higher than the figure determined by the LVT notwithstanding that there was no appeal from the respondents.

Procedure

16–13 In *Earl Cadogan v Sportelli* [2007] 1 E.G.L.R. 153 at para. 117, the Lands Tribunal held that it was entitled to lay down principles of practice, including matters of quantification, to which regard should be had by first-tier tribunals; in that case the deferment rate applicable to properties throughout the country. This approach was approved by the Court of Appeal: [2007] EWCA Civ 1042, *per* Carnwath L.J. at paras 93–99.

Costs

Also introduced to Wales with effect from March 30, 2004. The Order is at   **16–14**
Appendix 2S.

Add to end of first sentence: There is no right of appeal to the Court of Appeal
from the refusal of the Lands Tribunal to grant permission to appeal from the
LVT: *R (Sinclair Gardens Investments (Kensington) Ltd) v Lands Tribunal*
[2005] EWCA Civ 1305; [2006] 1 E.G.L.R. 7. Moreover, as the Court of Appeal
held in that case, whilst judicial review of the Lands Tribunal's decision not to
grant permission would lie in theory, it would only be exercised in exceptional
circumstances.

Appeal to the Court of Appeal   **16–15**

Footnote 154: *Gallagher* is spelt with a "g".

There have been further such appeals in *Fattal v Keepers and Governors of the
Free Grammar School of John Lyon* [2004] EWCA Civ 1530; [2005] 1 W.L.R.
803 and *Cadogan v Sportelli* [2007] EWCA Civ 1042.

CHAPTER 17

MISCELLANEOUS

2.—POWER OF COURT

In *Murrell v Bickenhall Engineering Ltd* (unreported, 1994) the Court of Appeal   **17–07**
held that there was a discretion whether or not to make an order under s. 20(6).
In a case where the tenant "had presented wholly false claims and had lied
throughout the proceedings" the discretion should be exercised in favour of
making a debarring order. The decision of the judge below, that no order should
be made because that would have barred the tenant for good, in view of the short
unexpired term of his lease, was reversed.

4.—MISSING LANDLORD

Footnote 101: The commencement date for Wales is March 31, 2004. The Order   **17–15**
is at Appendix 2S.

CHAPTER 19

PLACES OF WORSHIP

Rights under the Act

In *Acton v Trustees of Birmingham South West Circuit Methodist Churches*   **19–07**
Manses Trust [2006] 3 E.G.L.R. 101, the Lands Tribunal held that a notice to
treat served under the 1920 Act, which the tenant had sought to withdraw, was
not validly withdrawn. It would have to have been withdrawn within six weeks
of a claim, by virtue of s. 31 of the Land Compensation Act 1961, and a valid
claim was made more than six weeks before the purported withdrawal.

Marriage value or tenant's bid

Lambe v Secretary of State for War was approved by the House of Lords in   **19–10**
Waters v Welsh Development Agency [2004] 1 W.L.R. 1304, *per* Lord Nicholls of
Birkenhead at para. 37.

In *Union of Welsh Independents Incorporated* (unreported, 2007), the Lands
Tribunal assessed compensation in a case where the landlord could not be found.
The bulk of the compensation was made up of marriage value.

CHAPTER 20

THE RIGHT TO COLLECTIVE ENFRANCHISEMENT

At the time of writing this Second Supplement, the RTE company provisions **20–01** under the Commonhold and Leasehold Reform Act 2002 have still not been brought into force, nor has even a provisional date been set for their commencement.

Footnotes 10 and 13: The right to manage came into force in Wales on March 31, 2004: The Commonhold and Leasehold Reform Act 2002 (Commencement No.2 and Savings) (Wales) Order 2004 SI 2004/669 (W62).

2.—Property Included in the Claim

Footnote 27: The *Lynari* case is now reported, with the parties' names trans- **20–05** posed, at [2003] 3 E.G.L.R. 147.

Acquisition of leasehold interests

Footnote 41: The *Crean Davidson* case was agreed to be correct on this point in **20–08** *Cadogan v Search Guarantees Plc* [2005] 1 All E.R. 280; [2004] 1 W.L.R. 2768 at para. 4 *per* Laddie J.

However, there is an alternative construction of s. 2, which would avoid this anomalous consequence. As explained in paragraph 20–09, s. 2(4) of the 1993 Act excludes from acquisition certain premises demised by the headlease. These include a flat not held by a qualifying tenant: see s. 2(4)(a). In its context, the "qualifying tenant" referred to in s. 2(4)(a) appears to refer back to a qualifying tenant whose lease is inferior to that held by the headlessee: s. 2(2). Accordingly, the headlease would not be acquired by the participating tenants insofar as it demises a flat which is not subject to a long sub-lease. That construction would seem to be preferable, and more in line with the presumed intention of the draftsman. It is also consistent with the approach in *Cadogan v Search Guarantees Plc* [2004] 1 W.L.R. 2768, referred to in para. 4–04.

Add to Footnote 41: That which was agreed in the *Crean Davidson* case was decided by the High Court. In *Maurice v Hollow-Ware Products Ltd* [2005] EWHC 815 (Ch); [2005] 2 E.G.L.R. 71 it was held that the lessee of a block of 28 flats was the qualifying tenant of each flat for the purposes of Chapter 2, and could claim individual new leases of each flat. The landlord's argument that practical conveyancing difficulties would be caused in that event, such that the draftsman could not have intended to include within the definition of qualifying tenant the lessee of a whole building, was rejected. Deputy Judge Donaldson Q.C. held, on the contrary, that ss. 39(4) and 101(3) of the 1993 Act made specific provision for leases where more than a single flat was demised. However, in *Howard de Walden Estates Ltd v Aggio* [2007] EWCA Civ 499; [2007] 3 W.L.R. 542, the Court of Appeal (hearing two appeals) overruled *Maurice v Hollow-Ware Products Ltd.* It held that a headlessee whose lease demised not only one or more flats, but also common parts could not be a qualifying tenant. The Act lacked any clear provisions to deal with the terms of a new lease to be granted to such a tenant, which indicated that Parliament had not intended a head lessee to be a qualifying tenant. In July 2007, the House of Lords granted the tenants in both appeals leave to appeal, and the appeals are pending.

20–09   A lease of the surface of, and the airspace above, the flat roof of a block is a lease of common parts, and is liable to acquisition under s. 2(1)(b). The roof space was required for the proper management of the roof, and proper management would not be possible were the lessee to build flats or place mobile phone masts upon it: *Kintyre Ltd v Romeomarch Property Management Ltd* [2006] 1 E.G.L.R. 67, Land Registry Deputy Adjudicator.

CHAPTER 21

PREMISES QUALIFYING

1.—"SELF-CONTAINED BUILDING"

Add: In *Long Acre Securities Ltd v Karet* [2004] EWHC 442 (Ch); [2005] Ch. 61, **21–02**
it was held that more than one building could be the subject of a notice under Part
1 of the Landlord and Tenant Act 1987 provided the occupants of the qualifying
flats in each building shared the use of the same appurtenant premises. The
decision is a controversial one, and has been the subject of academic criticism:
see article by D. Readings in the New Law Journal April 23, 2004 at p. 622. As
that article points out the deputy Judge did not have the advantage of hearing any
argument against the landlord. However, the decision can readily be distinguished as far as the 1993 Act is concerned, since the 1987 Act contains no
definition of building.

Add: In what is believed to be the first case to consider these provisions, **21–03**
Oakwood Court (Holland Park) Ltd v Daejan Properties Ltd [2007] 1 E.G.L.R.
121, it was held that a part of a building excluding a boiler house supplying hot
water, etc. to both it and a neighbouring block was not a self-contained part of a
building. H.H. Judge Marshall Q.C. held that the appropriate approach was to
take the following five steps:

   (a) identify the services provided to occupiers of the enfranchising part
      which are in issue because they are not independently provided;

   (b) consider whether those services can be provided to the enfranchising
      part independently of the provision of the same service(s) to the remain-
      der of the building;

   (c) ascertain the works required to separate the respective parts of the
      services supplying the enfranchising part and the remainder of the
      building, so that such services would thereafter be supplied to each such
      part independently of the other;

   (d) assess the interruption to the latter services (*i.e.* those serving the
      neighbouring block) which carrying out those works would entail; and
      finally

(e) decide whether this is "significant" within the meaning of the subsection.

The first issue is a question of plain fact. The second, third and fourth are
matters of expert evidence. The fifth is a question of construction of the Act and
the application of that construction as a matter of fact and degree. In considering
what is "significant", the emphasis is on the duration of the interruption and the
seriousness of the effect of any prospective interruption is also a factor to be
taken into account. The requirement for separate services was held not to be
fulfilled where the relevant services were to be provided to the enfranchising part
by some separate means, different from the existing means and not in existence
or available.

Add to Footnote 9: In *Holding and Management (Solitaire) Ltd—1–16 Finland
St RTM Co Ltd* [2007] P.L.S.C.S. 214, the Lands Tribunal considered the
identical provisions in a right to manage claim under s. 72 of the Commonhold
and Leasehold Reform Act 2002. It was held that the 1967 Act provisions in s.
2(2) of that Act relating to overlapping parts, as interpreted in *Malekshad,* did not
assist the tenants. There must be a clear vertical division of the building, subject
only to a possible de minimis deviation. A deviation in the vertical plane, leaving
two per cent of the floor area below the neighbouring part of the building meant
that there was no vertical division.

2.—Two or More Flats Held by Qualifying Tenants

21–04 Add to Footnote 20: That which was agreed in the *Crean Davidson* case has now
been considered by the higher courts. In *Maurice v Hollow-Ware Products Ltd*
[2005] EWHC 815 (Ch); [2005] 2 E.G.L.R. 71, it was held by the High Court
that the lessee of a block of 28 flats was the qualifying tenant of each flat for the
purposes of Chapter 2, and could claim individual new leases of each flat. The
landlord's argument that practical conveyancing difficulties would be caused in
that event, such that the draftsman could not have intended to include within the
definition of qualifying tenant the lessee of a whole building, was rejected.
Deputy Judge Donaldson Q.C. held, on the contrary, that ss. 39(4) and 101(3) of
the 1993 Act made specific provision for leases where more than a single flat was
demised. However, in *Howard de Walden Estates Ltd v Aggio* [2007] EWCA Civ
499; [2007] 3 W.L.R. 542, the Court of Appeal (hearing two appeals) overruled
Maurice v Hollow-Ware Products Ltd. It held that a headlessee whose lease
demised not only one or more flats, but also common parts could not be a
qualifying tenant. The Act lacked any clear provisions to deal with the terms of
a new lease to be granted to such a tenant, which indicated that Parliament had
not intended a head lessee to be a qualifying tenant. In July 2007, the House of
Lords granted the tenants in both appeals leave to appeal, and the appeals are
pending.

4.—EXCLUDED PREMISES

(1) Part non-residential use

Add to Footnote 35: In *WHRA RTM Co Ltd v Gaingold Ltd* [2006] 1 E.G.L.R.   **21–08**
81, the Lands Tribunal held that residential accommodation used by staff
employed by the occupier of commercial premises was nevertheless occupied for
residential purposes under paragraph 1(2) of Schedule 6 to the 2002 Act (*i.e.* the
equivalent provision to s. 4(2) of the 1993 Act in the right to manage regime).

Add: In *Indiana Investments Ltd v Taylor* [2004] 3 E.G.L.R. 63, County Court,   **21–09—**
Judge Cooke held that the correct exercise was that set out here, *i.e.* to disregard   **21–10**
the area of any common parts on both sides of the equation. In considering a
number of disputed areas, it was held that coal vaults under the pavement, which
were unconnected to the building, were to be disregarded. However, other vaults,
which had been incorporated as part of a residential flat, were to be counted as
part of the building and as part of the residential space. An outdoor area, with
three, but not four, walls, was not part of the building. A party wall dividing
commercial from residential areas on lower floors was common parts. However,
on the upper floors where it had been pierced to facilitate the lateral conversion
of flats, the wall was residential.

In *Marine Court (St Leonards on Sea) Freeholders Ltd v Rother District
Investments Ltd* [2007] P.L.S.C.S. 199, H.H. Judge Hollis held (i) common parts
included any part of the building which is not let and is used in common by more
than one occupier. They do not have to be common to both residential and
commercial occupants of the building. Thus, for example, a corridor leading only
to two commercial units is excluded from measurement, because it is common
parts; and (ii) in measuring the internal floor area of areas occupied for residential
purposes, balconies forming the demise of flats are included where they are
recessed into the flat or at least partially enclosed. By contrast, other balconies
open to the sky and largely to the sides were excluded from the measurement of
internal floor areas.

(2) Resident landlord

Add after the second paragraph: In *Slamon v Planchon* [2004] EWCA Civ 799;   **21–13**
[2005] Ch. 142; [2004] 4 All E.R. 407, the Court of Appeal has held that the
resident landlord needs to have held the same interest throughout in order for the
exception to apply. A freehold owner who, for part of the period since the
conversion had been carried out, held the freehold as beneficial owner under a
trust, did not fall within the exclusion. It was accepted that the decision could
cause anomalies where properties were held jointly by members of the same
family, but it was determined that the statutory wording was clear.

CHAPTER 22

TENANCIES QUALIFYING

1.—LONG LEASES

Add to footnote 9: Since the Civil Partnership Act 2004 came into force on **22–02** December 5, 2005, a tenancy taking effect under s. 149(6) of the Law of Property Act 1925 includes a lease terminable after the formation of a civil partnership. The exclusion under s. 7(2) now includes in addition a termination notice capable of being given at any time after the formation of a civil partnership where the tenancy can be terminated on that basis.

In paragraph (c) the cross reference should be to paragraph 3–07 not 3–08.

Paragraph (e): Section 7(1)(d), which deals with shared-ownership leases, is a left over from the unamended 1993 Act, which as originally enacted excluded long leases let otherwise than at a low rent. Section 7(1)(d) became otiose when the exclusion of long leases otherwise than at a low rent was removed by the 2002 Act, but Parliament omitted to delete it from the remaining provisions of the 1993 Act: *Brick Farm Management Ltd v Richmond Housing Partnership Ltd* [2005] 1 W.L.R. 3934, *per* Stanley Burnton J., at para. 23. It is considered that a shared-ownership lease granted for a term of more than 21 years now falls within s. 7(1)(a), regardless of the tenant's total share.

Exceptions

Add: In *The Bishopsgate Foundation v Curtis* [2004] 3 E.G.L.R. 57, County Ct, **22–05** Judge Cooke held that the tenant of a flat created in a former industrial building demised to be used for live/work purposes was a qualifying tenant, where there was no significant business user such as to bring the tenancy within Pt 2 of the Landlord and Tenant Act 1954. The user provision did not require the tenant positively to occupy for business as well as residential purposes. The case is discussed in an article by N. Rees on p. 148 of the Estates Gazette of October 9, 2004.

Charitable housing trust **22–07**

In *Brick Farm Management Ltd v Richmond Housing Partnership Ltd* [2005] 1 W.L.R. 3934, it was held that, for the purposes of s. 5(2)(b), the housing accommodation provided by a charitable housing trust was restricted to the social housing it provided. That did not include flats let on long leases where the trust had acquired the freehold from a local authority which had granted the long leases under the right to buy provisions of the Housing Act 1985. The fact that some flats in the building were let by the trust on assured tenancies did not prevent the qualifying tenants from making a collective enfranchisement claim.

It should be noted that it is possible for a charitable housing trust to grant a long lease at a premium: *Joseph Rowntree Memorial Trust Housing Association Ltd v Attorney-General* [1983] Ch. 159.

CHAPTER 23

QUALIFYING TENANTS AND LANDLORDS

4.—LANDLORDS

Footnote 70: The commencement date for Wales is March 31, 2004. The Order **23–14** is at Appendix 2S.

CHAPTER 24

PARTICIPATING TENANTS AND NOMINEE PURCHASER (THE RTE COMPANY AND PARTICIPATION IN A CLAIM)

1.—PARTICIPATING TENANTS

It is considered that the issue as to whether or not a sufficient number of qualifying tenants has given the initial notice is determined once and for all at the "relevant date". Consequently, any change in the participating tenants thereafter does not affect the validity of the claim. However, difficult questions may arise as to who should be regarded as participating tenants for the purpose of calculating the marriage value if the number of participating tenants is reduced after the giving of the initial notice: see, *e.g. Erkman v Earl Cadogan* (unreported, 2007, LVT), which is subject to a pending appeal. The problem arises in consequence of the failure of the draftsman to reconsider the provisions of s. 14 when the valuation date was changed to the date of the giving of the initial notice by the 2002 Act. **24–01**

2.—NOMINEE PURCHASER

Add to Footnote 55: A form of Trust Deed, drafted by His Honour John Hicks Q.C., is now published in Precedents for the Conveyancer (Sweet & Maxwell) paragraph 19–E7, at pp. 9861–9868. **24–09**

3.—RTE COMPANIES

At the time of writing this Second Supplement, the RTE company provisions under the Commonhold and Leasehold Reform Act 2002 have still not been brought into force, nor has even a provisional date been set for their commencement. **24–15—24–23**

Participating members

Footnote 106: the word "paw" should read "law". **24–20**

CHAPTER 25

PROCEDURE—PRELIMINARY INQUIRIES AND INITIAL NOTICE

2.—INITIAL NOTICE

Illustrations

(3) *House divided into three flats*
Add to Footnote 46: It also requires not less than one-half of the qualifying **25–07**
tenants to have satisfied the repealed residence condition. It is considered that
this oversight is so obvious, and applying it would produce such an anomalous
result, that it would be ignored by the court.

Contents of notice

(c) *Acquisition of leasehold interest and leaseback*
The last words of this paragraph should read "(under Part III of Schedule 9)." **25–09**

(d) *Proposed purchase prices*
Add to Footnote 62: It should be noted that the price for the freehold interest **25–10**
includes the landlord's 50 per cent share of the marriage value: see paragraph
2(1)(a) of Schedule 6 to the 1993 Act. This is then shared between the freeholder
and any intermediate landlords in proportion to the value of their respective
interests: paragraph 9 of Schedule 6. It sometimes happens that the tenants or the
landlord (in the counter-notice) share the marriage value in the figures proposed
in the initial notice and counter-notice. If this is done, it should be stated in terms
to avoid later confusion.

Add to Footnote 64: The decision in *Cadogan v Morris* has been reconsidered
by the Court of Appeal in *9 Cornwall Crescent London Ltd v Royal Borough of
Kensington and Chelsea* [2005] EWCA Civ 324; [2006] 1 W.L.R. 1186. The case
involved a challenge to the validity of a landlord's counter-notice on the ground
that the proposed figure was unrealistically high. It was held (1) that there was
no requirement that the figure in a counter-notice should be realistic or subject to
any other qualification; (2) the reason for this was that, unlike in the case of the
tenants' notice, the figure specified could never become the price by default; (3)

obiter in the case of a tenants' notice, the only requirement for the proposal figure was that it should be made in good faith; that it could be an opening shot in negotiations, and that it did not have to be justified by valuation evidence. The test in *Mount Cook Land Ltd v Rosen,* referred to in Footnote 64, was held to be incorrect.

Add to Footnote 65: In *Woodrolfe Park Freehold Ltd v Drake-Lewis* [2002] EWCA Civ 1586, Mance L.J. refused to grant the landlord permission to appeal from the county court judge's ruling that an initial notice was valid. The landlord had failed to serve a counter-notice, and challenged the validity of the s. 13 notice on the ground that the proposed price was, applying *Cadogan v Morris,* wholly unrealistic. The tenants' proposal was £16,000 and evidence was called to justify a valuation of £16,897. The landlord's valuer gave evidence that the price should be £222,750. Whilst Mance L.J. agreed that it seemed surprising that the marriage value contended for by the tenants was so low, it was not suggested that their valuation was not *bona fide.* The court could not say that it was unrealistic in the extreme sense which would be required to come within the principle elaborated in *Cadogan v Morris.*

Footnote 74: In the third line, "March 7" should have been stated instead of "March 8".

Inaccuracy or misdescription

25–12 Add to Footnote 91: In *Malekshad v Howard de Walden Estates Ltd (No.2)* [2003] EWHC 3106 (Ch); [2004] 1 W.L.R. 862, a case under the equivalent provision under the 1967 Act (*i.e.* paragraph 6(3) of Schedule 3), Neuberger J. held that the inclusion of property which ought not to have been included invalidated the notice unless the notice was appropriately amended. Although there is a discretion, the court would normally grant leave to amend a notice unconditionally unless the landlord could establish any relevant prejudice as a result of having been served with an invalid notice.

In *Oakwood Court (Holland Park) Ltd v Daejan Properties Ltd* [2007] 1 E.G.L.R. 121, it was held that paragraph 15(2) cannot be read purposively to permit amendments in cases other than those specified. It applies only where the initial notice either specifies property or an interest that the claimant is not entitled to acquire under ss. 1 or 2 or fails to specify property or an interest that the claimant is entitled to acquire.

25–13 **Signature**

In *City & Country Properties Ltd v Plowden Investments Ltd* [2007] L. & T.R. 15, it was held in the county court that a company must sign a s. 42 notice by executing it is accordance with s. 36A of the Companies Act 1985, *i.e.* by affixing its company's seal or arranging for it to be signed by two directors or by a director and the company secretary. If correct, the decision would apply to the signature of an initial notice by a company participating tenant. It is debatable whether this decision is correct, given that the Act does not require 'execution' of a notice but only signature. Since a company is an artificial person, it would seem that it can sign a notice by authorising someone to do so on its behalf.

Freehold   **25–15**

Add to Footnote 117: In *BCLA Ltd v Demetriou* (unreported, 2006), a Land Registry Deputy Adjudicator (Ms. Stevens-Hoare) allowed the registration of two 999-year leases of flats, granted by way of surrender and re-grant, where a s. 13 initial notice had been protected by a caution. The caution remained in place.

A lease of the surface of, and the airspace above, the flat roof of a block is a lease of common parts, and is liable to acquisition under s. 2(1)(b). The roof space was required for the proper management of the roof, and proper management would not be possible were the lessee to build flats or place mobile phone masts upon it. Consequently, the lease was void under s. 19 and would not be registered: *Kintyre Ltd v Romeomarch Property Management Ltd* [2006] 1 E.G.L.R. 67, Land Registry Deputy Adjudicator.

Leasehold

Add to Footnote 138: In *Malekshad v Howard de Walden Estates Ltd (No.2)*   **25–17** [2003] EWHC 3106 (Ch); [2004] 1 W.L.R. 862, a case under the equivalent provision under the 1967 Act (*i.e.* paragraph 3(1) of Schedule 3), Neuberger J. held that making a claim had the effect of prolonging the tenancy. It would appear, therefore, that if a qualifying tenant's lease demises other flats, the whole lease is continued by this provision. Difficult questions (*e.g.* as to responsibility for management of the building) arise if the qualifying tenant participating in the claim is the headlessee of the building (see paragraph 20–08 above). Moreover, if a claim to enfranchise is ineffective, and a new claim is made during the three-month period, the relevant tenant will be a qualifying tenant during that three-month period.

No further notice

In *Sinclair Gardens Investments (Kensington) Ltd v Poets Chase Freehold Co*   **25–18** *Ltd* [2007] EWHC 1776 (Ch); [2007] 32 E.G. 89 (CS), the tenants purported to serve a section 13 initial notice, but it failed to comply with the requirements of s. 13(3) and was invalid. The landlord's counter-notice disputed the validity of the notice. It was held by Morgan J. that the tenants were entitled to treat their purported initial notice as a nullity and serve a further, valid, section 13 notice. The prohibition in s. 13(9) on serving a further notice within 12 months of a withdrawal or deemed withdrawal did not apply in these circumstances. The tenants were not estopped from asserting the invalidity of the original notice.

CHAPTER 26

PROCEDURE FOLLOWING INITIAL NOTICE

1.—REVERSIONER'S INVESTIGATION RIGHTS

Evidence of tenant's rights

Footnote 19: The *Raymere* case is now reported at [2004] Ch. 29. **26–03**

Footnote 23: The commencement date for Wales is March 31, 2004. The Regulations are at Appendix 2T.

2.—NEW AGREEMENTS BY NOMINEE PURCHASERS

Add to Footnote 26: Section 126(2) of the 2002 Act, amending s. 18(1) of the   **26–04** 1993 Act, was brought into force on February 28, 2005: The Commonhold and Leasehold Reform Act 2002 (Commencement No.5 and Saving and Transitional Provision) Order 2004 set out at Appendix 2W. This applies to England only. It was brought into force in Wales on May 31, 2005: The Commonhold and Leasehold Reform Act 2002 (Commencement No.3 and Savings and Transitional Provision)(Wales) Order 2005 (SI 2005 No.1353 (W.101)), set out at Appendix 2Y.

It should be noted that the other RTE provisions of the 2002 Act have still not been brought into force.

The revised provisions contain a possible difficulty. A contract is only entered into after all the terms of acquisition have been agreed. If an agreement within the meaning of s. 18 is made after the date when the terms of acquisition have been agreed but before a contract is entered into, in the absence of an agreement to revise the previously agreed terms, it would seem that the only remedy would be for the reversioner to refuse to enter into the contract, apply (or let the nominee purchaser apply) to the court for an order under s. 24(3) (as to which, see paragraph 26–10), and rely on the s. 18 agreement as being a change of circumstances under s. 24(4)(b) (as to which, see paragraph 26–11).

Add to Footnote 34: However, in *Cadogan v Sportelli* [2007] EWCA Civ 1042, the Court of Appeal held that hope value is not to be included in valuations under the 1993 Act, and also indicated that s. 18 now appears to have little purpose: see Carnwath L.J. at para. 56. A petition for leave to appeal to the House of Lords is expected.

3.—THE COUNTER-NOTICE

26–05 Add at end: In *7 Strathray Gardens Ltd v Pointstar Shipping and Finance Ltd* [2004] EWCA Civ 1669; [2005] 1 E.G.L.R. 53, the Court of Appeal held the failure to state that the specified premises were not within the area of an estate management scheme under s. 70 of the 1993 Act did not invalidate a counter-notice. The requirement was held to be directory, rather than mandatory, applying a line of authority culminating in *Tudor v M25 Group Ltd* [2004] 1 W.L.R. 2319, a decision of the Court of Appeal on s. 54 of the Landlord and Tenant Act 1987. In the case of any failure to comply with a statutory requirement, it is necessary to consider whether the draftsman intended the failure to render the whole process a nullity. The inference from the leading judgment of Arden L.J. is that, had the specified premises been within a scheme, the counter-notice would have been invalid had it not so stated. The judgments left open the question whether tenants have a potential claim for damages for breach of statutory duty. The House of Lords refused a petition to leave to appeal. It should be noted that the House of Lords has subsequently held that the rigid mandatory/directory distinction has outlived its usefulness (*R v Soneji* [2006] 1 A.C. 340, *per* Lord Steyn at para. 23): "the emphasis ought to be on the consequences of non-compliance, and posing the question whether Parliament can fairly be taken to have intended total invalidity".

In *Riverside Millbrook v Lampard* (unreported, 2005, Guildford County Court) H.H. Judge Reid Q.C. held that a counter-notice which specified a reason for not admitting the right which was bad in law was nevertheless a valid counter-notice.

In *Sinclair Gardens Investments (Kensington) Ltd v Poets Chase Freehold Co Ltd* [2007] EWHC 1776 (Ch), the validity of a counter-notice under s. 21 of the Act which simply challenged the validity of an initial notice, rather than give a reason for not admitting the tenants' right by reference to the eligibility criteria was left open: Morgan J. at para. 63.

Counter-notice admitting the right

26–06 Add to Footnote 52: The decision in *Cadogan v Morris* has been reconsidered by the Court of Appeal in *9 Cornwall Crescent London Ltd v Royal Borough of Kensington and Chelsea* [2005] EWCA Civ 324; [2006] 1 W.L.R. 1186. The case involved a challenge to the validity of a landlord's counter-notice on the ground that the proposed figure was unrealistically high. It was held (1) that there was no requirement that the figure in a counter-notice should be realistic or subject to any other qualification; (2) the reason for this was that, unlike in the case of the tenants' notice, the figure specified could never become the price by default.

If the counter-notice does not contain a leaseback proposal, the opportunity will have been missed; it will be too late to do so subsequently: *Cawthorne v Hamdan* [2007] EWCA Civ 6; [2007] Ch. 187.

Add: In *Sinclair Gardens Investments (Kensington) Ltd v Poets Chase Freehold*   **26–07**
Co Ltd [2007] EWHC 1776 (Ch), the validity of a counter-notice under s. 21 of
the Act which simply challenged the validity of an initial notice, rather than give
a reason for not admitting the tenants' right by reference to the eligibility criteria
was left open: Morgan J. at para. 63.

Proceedings where dispute

(2) *Negative counter-notice*
Footnote 83: The time for appealing is not four weeks from the date of the order,   **26–08**
but is now 21 days after the date of the decision, or such period as may be
directed by the lower court: CPR, r.52.4(2).

A purported further counter-notice which contests the tenants' right to enfranchise is invalid: *Brick Farm Management Ltd v Richmond Housing Partnership
Ltd (No.2)* [2006] 2 E.G.L.R. 46. The court has already declared that the
participating tenants are entitled to enfranchise, and the landlord does not have
another opportunity to challenge the right. Moreover, the further counter-notice
must be served by the date specified by the court. There is no jurisdiction to apply
to the court to extend the time: *ibid*. The date specified by the court becomes the
new statutory time limit. It was held that CPR, r.3.1(2)(a) did not confer a
discretion to extend the time.

Security for costs
Add at end: But see paragraphs 28–23 for a case where security for costs was
refused.

Applications where terms are in dispute or no contract is entered into
Add to Footnote 103: In *9 Cornwall Crescent London Ltd v Royal Borough of*   **26–10**
Kensington and Chelsea [2005] EWCA Civ 324; [2006] 1 W.L.R. 1186, it had
been held, *obiter*, by the trial judge that the matters in dispute are defined as the
range between the proposal in the initial notice and the counter-proposal in the
counter-notice. This seems questionable in that s. 24 does not expressly so limit
the tribunal's jurisdiction. The Court of Appeal did not follow the trial judge's
holding on this point, *per* Auld L.J. at para. 6, although Arden L.J. expressed no
view on it [para. 76].

Add to Footnote 118: In *Sinclair Gardens Investments Kensington Ltd v Eardley*   **26–11**
Crescent No. 75 Ltd (unreported, 2006, Lands Tribunal) H.H. Judge Huskinson
held that an LVT could determine disputed terms at a later hearing, even if the
original application had only idenitfied the purchase price and costs as being in
dispute.

Add to (b) on p. 428: In *Castlegroom v Enoch (No.2)* [2003] 3 E.G.L.R. 46,
the leasehold valuation tribunal held that there was no jurisdiction under s. 24(4)
of the 1993 Act to increase the price payable. An increase in property prices since
the price was agreed was not a change in circumstances within the meaning of
s. 24(4)(b).

CHAPTER 27

PURCHASE PRICE AND TERMS

1.—VALUATION DATE

Section 126(1) of the 2002 Act, changing the valuation date to the relevant date, **27–02** was brought into force on February 28, 2005: Commonhold and Leasehold Reform Act 2002 (Commencement No.5, Savings and Transitional Provisions) Order 2004. This applies to England only. The original transitional provision did not deal with the situation where an initial notice is served before the commencement date. That omission was pointed out by the authors and rectified by The Commonhold and Leasehold Reform Act 2002 (Commencement No.5 and Saving and Transitional Provision) (Amendment) (England) Order 2005 (SI 2005/193). The alteration in valuation date does not now have effect as regards initial notices given before February 28, 2005 or applications made under s. 26 of the 1993 Act before that date. The Commencement No.5 Order as amended is set out at Appendix 2W. It was brought into force in Wales on May 31, 2005: The Commonhold and Leasehold Reform Act 2002 (Commencement No.3 and Savings and Transitional Provision)(Wales) Order 2005 (SI 2005 No.1353 (W.101)), set out at Appendix 2Y.

In *Blendcrown Ltd v Church Commissioners for England* [2004] 1 E.G.L.R. 143, the Lands Tribunal (P. Clarke FRICS) held on the facts of that case that the valuation date was the date when the counter-notice was served. A counter-notice referring to the fact that provisions were to be included in the conveyance under s. 34 and Schedule 7 was simply a statement of the consequences of a collective enfranchisement claim. Since no specific provisions were included in the counter-notice, there was no issue as to what freehold interest was to be acquired. Permission to appeal was refused by the Court of Appeal (Waller and Dyson L.JJ.), which held that the Lands Tribunal's decision was correct: [2004] EWCA Civ 536.

2.—THE PRICE

Freehold owned by same person

Four main assumptions
(b) In *Earl Cadogan v Cadogan Square Limited* (unreported 2007) the LVT held **27–04** that only a section 42 notice which has been served by a non-participating tenant before the relevant date is to be taken into account in valuing the freeholder's

interest. It may be however that a later section 42 notice constitutes a change of circumstances capable of affecting a vesting order within s. 24(4)(b)(i). An appeal is pending.

Hope value

27–06   In *Blendcrown Ltd v Church Commissioners for England* [2004] 1 E.G.L.R. 143, the Lands Tribunal awarded hope value amounting to five per cent of the possible marriage value of non-participating tenants: para. [79]. It was said at paragraph [78] that the greater the number of non-participating tenants the greater the chances of future applications for lease extensions and the realisation of hope value. However, the whole question of whether hope value could be included was reconsidered in *Cadogan v Sportelli* [2007] 1 E.G.L.R. 153. It was held that the exclusion of the tenants from the market in paragraph 3 of Schedule 6 to the 1993 Act meant that hope value could not be taken into account in valuing the freeholder's interest: paras 98–108. The Court of Appeal dismissed an appeal against the Lands Tribunal's decision on hope value: [2007] EWCA Civ 1042. A petition for leave to appeal to the House of Lords is expected.

Yield

27–08   In *Blendcrown Ltd v Church Commissioners for England* [2004] 1 E.G.L.R. 143, the Lands Tribunal (P. Clarke FRICS) held that previous tribunal decisions on yield are not evidence in themselves and are no substitute for evidence. Accordingly, no weight was given to them: paragraph [53]. In *Cadogan v Sportelli* [2007] 1 E.G.L.R. 153, it was held by the Lands Tribunal that, in determining the deferment rate, evidence of open market sales of freehold reversions did not provide good evidence because the sales were tainted by 1993 Act rights. After a detailed consideration of other financial evidence the Tribunal determined that the deferment rate should be five per cent, and that that rate should apply generally to flats regardless of location, subject to exceptional factors. The location of the flat would usually be reflected in the open market values used in calculating the price and should not influence the deferment rate. The Court of Appeal has dismissed the appeals against the Lands Tribunal's decision on deferment rate: [2007] EWCA Civ 1042. This is effectively binding guidance for properties within the Prime Central London area. Outside that area, it remains open to valuers to seek to argue for a different rate, using five per cent as the starting point: *per* Carnwath L.J. at para. 102.

The rate used to capitalise the freeholder's rental income should usually be considered separately from the deferment rate: *Nicholson v Goff* [2007] 1 E.G.L.R. 83, where at para. 9 the Lands Tribunal listed the factors which would influence that rate. These were; (i) the length of the lease term; (ii) the security of recovery; (iii) the size of the ground rent (a larger ground rent being more attractive); (iv) whether there was provision for review of the ground rent and (v) if there were such provision, the nature of it.

Marriage value

27–09   Footnote 70: The amendments to the valuation date and to s. 18 of the 1993 Act made by s. 126 of the 2002 Act were brought into force on February 28, 2005:

Commonhold and Leasehold Reform Act 2002 (Commencement No.5, Savings and Transitional Provisions) Order 2004. This applies to England only. They was brought into force in Wales on May 31, 2005: The Commonhold and Leasehold Reform Act 2002 (Commencement No.3 and Savings and Transitional Provision)(Wales) Order 2005 (SI 2005 No.1353 (W.101)), set out at Appendix 2Y.

Since the RTE provisions introduced by ss. 121–124 of the 2002 Act have still not been brought into force, art. 4 of the English Order and art. 3(1) of the Welsh Order make a transitional provision. During the period beginning with February 28, 2005 (May 31, 2005 in Wales) and ending on the date when ss. 121–124 of the 2002 Act come into force, paragraph 4(2) of Schedule 6 to the 1993 Act has effect as if, for "participating tenants", there were substituted "persons who are participating tenants immediately before a binding contract is entered into in pursuance of the initial notice". This is equivalent to the amendment which will be made to paragraph 4(2) by paragraph 40(5) of Schedule 8 to the 2002 Act, that Schedule being introduced by s. 124 of the 2002 Act.

The authors have reconsidered their criticism of the drafting, as set out in the third paragraph on p. 440. It is considered that the fact that the increase in price which represents the marriage value must be based on the same assumptions as under paragraph 3(1) makes it clear that the relevant disregards apply throughout the calculation. The corresponding provision in Schedule 13 is distinguishable insofar as the definition of marriage value therein contains a specific direction to value the interest of the tenant under the existing lease. In consequence, it is necessary to set out the assumptions to be made in calculating that value.

The difficulties in deciding who are the participating tenants for the purpose of this provision is discussed in paragraph 24–01, above.

(i) *Criticism of definition*
Add after the first sentence of the second paragraph: By transitional provisions, **27–10** until the RTE provisions are brought into force, "participating member" is to be read as "participating tenant": see the 2002 Act Commencement No.1 Order, Schedule 2, paragraph 3.

Value of intermediate lease
In the lease of a block of flats there is often a caretaker's flat. The value of the **27–16** intermediate lease may reflect the right of the head lessee to recover a rent in respect of the caretaker's flat through the service charges levied on the other flat lessees. Whether or not such a rent is recoverable though the service charge, and thus ought to be reflected in the value of the headlease, will depend on the construction of the covenants in the leases. In *Cadogan v 44/46 Lower Sloane Street Management Co Ltd* (unreported, 2004), the Lands Tribunal held that no rent was recoverable in respect of the caretaker's flat. That case was distinguished in *Earl Cadogan v 27/29 Sloane Gardens Ltd* [2006] L. & T.R. 18, where the lease terms were materially different. The Court of Appeal refused to grant the freeholder permission to appeal in the latter case: [2006] EWCA Civ 1331.

CHAPTER 28

TERMINATION OR COMPLETION OF CLAIM

5.—CANCELLATION OF LAND CHARGE OR NOTICE

Footnote 56: The procedure relating to the registration and cancellation of notices **28–08** generally is now set out in paragraph 6.4 of Land Registry Practice Guide 27 (November 2006).

6.—COMPLETION AND CONVEYANCE

Vendor's lien   **28–12**
Now in paragraph 6.2.5 of the Land Registry Practice Guide 27 (November 2006).

Terms of conveyance
Footnote 93: Now in paragraph 6.2.1 of the Land Registry Practice Guide 27   **28–14** (November 2006).

Leases back
The notice must be contained in the counter-notice: s. 21(3)(a)(ii) and (7), see   **28–15** paragraph 26–06 and *Cawthorne v Hamdan* [2007] EWCA Civ 6; [2007] Ch. 187. The suggestion that a separate notice seeking a leaseback could be served at any time up to completion has been clearly disapproved of by the Court of Appeal in that case. The suggestion was based on the wording of paragraph 5(1) of Schedule 9, referring to a unit not "immediately before the appropriate time" being a flat let to a qualifying tenant. The Court of Appeal held that this wording required the flat to continue not to be let to a qualifying tenant up to completion, in order for the freeholder to be entitled to the leaseback he sought in the counter-notice. The only issue left open by that decision is whether a leaseback could be sought at a later date of a flat which is let to a qualifying tenant when the counter-notice is served, but subsequently ceases to be so let: *per* Lloyd L.J. at para.[31]. The judge thought the situation is unlikely to arise in practice.

73 Denmark Villas Hove Ltd v Elbaccush [2006] P.L.S.C.S. 164, in which Judge Simpkiss at Brighton County Court held that a reversioner could seek a voluntary leaseback after serving his counter-notice, is inconsistent with *Cawthorne v Hamdan* and therefore must be treated as wrongly decided on that point.

Footnote 119: Now in paragraph 6.2.8 of the Land Registry Practice Guide 27 (November 2006).

Terms of lease back

28–16   In *Midhage v 60 Coolhurst Road Ltd* [2007] 36 E.G. 302, the Lands Tribunal refused to allow the term in a leaseback to allow the freeholder to construct a car parking space in the front garden of the building containing the flats. The existing lease of all three flats in the building contained a mutually enforceable restrictive covenant against such parking. A covenant was, however, inserted so as to allow the freeholder to apply to the Lands Tribunal under s. 84 of the Law of Property Act 1925; had this not been included, the freeholder would have lost her accrued right to apply, since her existing lease had already run for 25 years (s. 84(12)).

Payments into court

28–20   Now in paragraph 6.2.6 of the Land Registry Practice Guide 27 (November 2006).

Costs

28–22   Footnote 222: The *Scottish Widows v Abbas* case was decided in 1999, not 2001.

CHAPTER 29

THE INDIVIDUAL RIGHT TO A NEW LEASE

Footnote 1: The commencement date for Wales is March 31, 2004. The Order is **29–01** at Appendix 2S.

The third sentence on p. 476 should start "Accordingly, it is necessary to refer to **29–02** Chapter 23 of this work where . . ."

Footnote 14 should refer to s. 130, not s. 127, of the 2002 Act. **29–03**

It is considered that if a lease is held on trust for two years, then a mere change **29–04** in the composition of the trustees during that period is not sufficient to require the new trustees to hold the lease for two years before a claim for a new lease can be made: *cf. Marsh v Gilbert* [1980] 2 E.G.L.R. 44. If a lease is vested in A and B as joint tenants, and then A becomes the sole tenant, either by survivorship on the death of B, or by a transfer of the lease to him alone, he may count the period of joint ownership as part of the two year period. As joint tenant, he had, in theory, the whole of the property: see e.g. Megarry & Wade, The Law of Real Property (6th ed.) paragraphs 9–002—9–007.

CHAPTER 30

NEW LEASE—PROCEDURE

2.—NOTICE OF CLAIM

Contents of notice

Footnote 41: The decision of the Court of Appeal (Tuckey L.J.) refusing permis- **30–07**
sion to appeal in the case of *Daejan Properties Ltd v Bellringer Investments Ltd*
has the neutral citation number [2002] EWCA Civ 663.

Footnote 42: The decision in *Cadogan v Morris* has been reconsidered by the
Court of Appeal in *9 Cornwall Crescent London Ltd v Royal Borough of
Kensington and Chelsea* [2005] EWCA Civ 324; [2006] 1 W.L.R. 1186. The case
involved a challenge to the validity of a landlord's counter-notice on the ground
that the proposed figure was unrealistically high. It was held (1) that there was
no requirement that the figure in a counter-notice should be realistic or subject to
any other qualification; (2) the reason for this was that, unlike in the case of the
tenants' notice, the figure specified could never become the price by default; (3)
obiter in the case of a tenants' notice, the only requirement for the proposal figure
was that it should be made in good faith; that it could be an opening shot in
negotiations, and that it did not have to be justified by valuation evidence. The
test in *Mount Cook Land Ltd v Rosen,* referred to in Footnote 42, was held to be
incorrect. The decision applies equally to a s. 42 notice.

Inaccuracies

Add to Footnote 58: In *Malekshad v Howard de Walden Estates Ltd (No.2)* **30–08**
[2004] 1 W.L.R. 862, a case under the equivalent provision under the 1967 Act
(*i.e.* paragraph 6(3) of Schedule 3), Neuberger J. held that the inclusion of
property which ought not to have been included invalidated the notice unless the
notice was appropriately amended. Although there is a discretion, the court
would normally grant leave to amend a notice unconditionally unless the landlord
could establish any relevant prejudice as a result of having been served with an
invalid notice.

In *Oakwood Court (Holland Park) Ltd v Daejan Properties Ltd* [2007] 1
E.G.L.R. 121, it was held in a case under the equivalent provision in a collective
enfranchisement claim that Schedule 3 paragraph 15(2) cannot be read purposively to permit amendments in cases other than those specified. It applies only

where the initial notice either specifes property or an interest that the claimant is not entitled to acquire under ss. 1 or 2 or fails to specify property or an interest that the claimant is entitled to acquire.

Signature
In *City & Country Properties Ltd v Plowden Investments Ltd* [2007] L. & T.R. 15, it was held in the county court that a company must sign a section 42 notice by executing it is accordance with s. 36A of the Companies Act 1985, *i.e.* by affixing its company's seal or arranging for it to be signed by two directors or by a director and the company secretary. It is debatable whether this decision is correct, given that the Act does not require "execution" of a notice but only signature. Since a company is an artificial person, it would seem that it can sign a notice by authorising someone to do so on its behalf.

Registration
Now in paragraph 6.4.1 of Land Registry Practice Guide 27 (November 2006).

The effect of serving a notice

Restriction on further notice

30–10 In *Sinclair Gardens Investments (Kensington) Ltd v Poets Chase Freehold Co Ltd* [2007] EWHC 1776 (Ch); [2007] 32 E.G. 89 (CS), the tenants purported to serve a section 13 initial notice, but it failed to comply with the requirements of s. 13(3) and was invalid. The landlord's counter-notice disputed the validity of the notice. It was held by Morgan J. that the tenants were entitled to treat their purported initial notice as a nullity and serve a further, valid, section 13 notice. The prohibition in s. 13(9) on serving a further notice within 12 months of a withdrawal or deemed withdrawal did not apply in these circumstances. The tenants were not estopped from asserting the invalidity of the orginial notice. It is clear that that decision applies equally to a section 42 notice.

Restriction on termination

30–11 Add to Footnote 94: In *Malekshad v Howard de Walden Estates Ltd (No.2)* [2004] 1 W.L.R. 862, a case under the equivalent provision under the 1967 Act (*i.e.* paragraph 3(1) of Sch. 3), Neuberger J. held that making a claim had the effect of prolonging the tenancy. An argument that, by analogy, if a qualifying tenant's lease demises other flats, the whole lease is continued by this provision was rejected in *Lay v Ackerman (No.2)* (unreported, 2006, Central London County Court). However, the tenant was given permission to appeal to the Court of Appeal and the appeal is pending. Difficult questions (*e.g.* as to responsibility for management of the building) arise if the qualifying tenant is the headlessee of the building (see paragraph 20–08, above). Moreover, if the claim is ineffective, and a new claim is made during the three-month period, the tenant will be the qualifying tenant during that three-month period.

3.—POST-NOTICE PROCEDURE

Assignment

Add to Footnote 99: In *Typeteam Ltd v Acton* (unreported, 2006, Central London   **30–13**
County Court) it was held that an assignment of the benefit of a section 42 notice
dated the same day as a Transfer of the lease in Form TR1 was effective, even
though the Transfer had yet to be registered at H.M. Land Registry. H.H. Judge
Cowell held that it was permissible to read s. 43(3) as referring to the assignment
or subsistence of interests either in law or in equity. The High Court has granted
the landlord permission to appeal, and an appeal is due to be heard in November
2007.

Footnote 102: *Money v Westholme* has now been given the neutral citation
[2003] EWCA Civ 1659.

Rights of landlord

Footnote 113: The commencement date for Wales is March 31, 2004. The   **30–14**
Regulations are set out at Appendix 2T.

Counter-notice

Footnote 120: In *Lay v Ackerman* [2004] H.L.R. 40, the Court of Appeal allowed   **30–15**
the landlords' appeal. It was held, applying the decision of the House of Lords
in *Mannai Investment Co Ltd v Eagle Star Life Assurance Co Ltd* [1997] A.C.
749, that the reasonable recipient of the counter-notice would have realised that
it came from the landlords, notwithstanding that they were incorrectly
described.

Add to Footnote 125: The decision in *Cadogan v Morris* has been reconsidered
by the Court of Appeal in *9 Cornwall Crescent London Ltd v Royal Borough of
Kensington and Chelsea* [2005] EWCA Civ 324; [2006] 1 W.L.R. 1186. The case
involved a challenge to the validity of a landlord's counter-notice on the ground
that the proposed figure was unrealistically high. It was held (1) that there was
no requirement that the figure in a counter-notice should be realistic or subject to
any other qualification; and (2) the reason for this was that, unlike in the case of
the tenants' notice, the figure specified could never become the price by
default.

Counter-notice not admitting the claim

Add: In *Bishopsgate Foundation v Curtis* [2004] 3 E.G.L.R. 57, H.H. Judge   **30–16**
Cooke held that if a landlord gives a counter-notice not admitting the right to a
new lease and starts proceedings under s. 46, he may not rely on any grounds
other than those stated in his counter-notice. Nevertheless, it is considered that
there is force in the landlord's argument (rejected by the judge) that the landlord
should not be in a worse position than if he had not served a counter-notice at all.
In the latter event, if the tenant had made an application under s. 49, the landlord
would be able to put forward any available argument to challenge the tenant's
right to a new lease. On the facts in that case, the landlord was not barred from
raising the arguments it wished to, because it was held that the reasons do not

have to be elaborated, only stated, and that had been done sufficiently in that case.

In *Riverside Millbrook v Lampard* (unreported, 2005, Guildford County Court) H.H. Judge Reid Q.C. held that a counter-notice which specified a reason for not admitting the right which was bad in law was nevertheless a valid counter-notice.

In *Sinclair Gardens Investments (Kensington) Ltd v Poets Chase Freehold Co Ltd* [2007] EWHC 1776 (Ch) the validity of a counter-notice under s. 21 of the Act which simply challenged the validity of an initial notice, rather than give a reason for not admitting the tenants' right by reference to the eligibility criteria was left open: Morgan J. at para. 63.

30–17   A purported further counter-notice which contests the tenant's right to a new lease is invalid: *Brick Farm Management Ltd v Richmond Housing Partnership Ltd (No.2)* [2006] 2 E.G.L.R. 46. The court has already declared that the tenant is so entitled, and the landlord does not have another opportunity to challenge the right. Moreover, the further counter-notice must be served by the date specified by the court. There is no jurisdiction to apply to the court to extend the time: *ibid.* The date specified by the court becomes the new statutory time limit. It was held that CPR, r.3.1(2)(a) does not confer a discretion to extend the time.

Redevelopment
30–18   The expression "any premises in which the flat is contained" refers to the building as a whole or any part of it which includes the tenant's flat, provided that that part is capable of being identified by a continuous line drawn on a three-dimensional plan of the building; there is no requirement that that part of the building be self-contained or that it be an existing recognisable unit: *Majorstake Ltd v Curtis* [2006] EWCA Civ. 1171; [2007] Ch. 300. Accordingly, it was held that the landlord could rely upon s. 47 where it intended to combine the flat with the one below it in the block to form a duplex apartment. The House of Lords granted the tenant leave to appeal (p. 317E), and the appeal is due to be heard in November 2007.

Counter-notice admitting the claim
30–20   Add to Footnote 159: In *9 Cornwall Crescent London Ltd v Royal Borough of Kensington and Chelsea* (unreported, Central London County Court, 2004), a collective enfranchisement case, it was held, *obiter,* that the matters in dispute are defined as the range between the proposal in the initial notice and the counter-proposal in the counter-notice. This seems questionable in that s. 48 does not expressly so limit the tribunal's jurisdiction. The Court of Appeal, [2005] EWCA Civ 324; [2006] 1 W.L.R. 1186, have not followed the trial Judge's holding on this point, *per* Auld L.J. at para. 6, although Arden L.J. expressed no view on it [para. 76].

Failure to serve a counter-notice
30–24   Add after the first sentence: The time for an application under s. 49 is six months from the date when the counter-notice should have been given. However, if an

application is made under s. 46 and then withdrawn, the landlord is treated as not having given a counter-notice: s. 46(2). In such a case, the date for a s. 49 application might have passed. The draftsman has not catered for this eventuality.

CHAPTER 31

TERMINATION AND SUSPENSION OF NEW LEASE CLAIM

Cancellation of land charge, etc.   **31–07**

Reference should now be made to paragraph 6.4.5 of the latest Land Registry
Practice Guide 27, dated November 2006, which is set out at Appendix 2Q of this
Supplement, and replaces Appendix 2Q in the main work.

CHAPTER 32

THE GRANT OF THE NEW LEASE

Changes to existing lease   **32–05**

Add to footnote 39: In *Gordon v Church Commissioners for England* (unreported, 2007, Lands Tribunal), H.H. Judge Huskinson, in a detailed consideration
of the provision and a number of LVT decisions, confirmed that s. 57(6) does not
allow the addition of the wholly new term in the absence of consent. The tenant
was accordingly unsuccessful in attempting to have included a new covenant
requiring the landlord to enforce covenants by tenants of other flats on the
landlord's estate if so requested.

Redevelopment   **32–20**

The expression "any premises in which the flat is contained" refers to the
building as a whole or any part of it which includes the tenant's flat, provided that
that part is capable of being identified by a continuous line drawn on a three-
dimensional plan of the building; there is no requirement that that part of the
building be self-contained or that it be an existing recognisable unit: *Majorstake
Ltd v Curtis* [2006] EWCA Civ 1171; [2007] Ch. 300. Accordingly, it was held
that the landlord could rely upon s. 47 where it intended to combine the flat with
the one below it in the block to form a duplex apartment. The House of Lords
granted the tenant leave to appeal (p. 317E), and the appeal is due to be heard in
November 2007. The wording in s. 61 is identical to that in s. 47, and it is
considered that this decision would clearly apply to a s. 61 application.

CHAPTER 33

NEW LEASE—PREMIUM

1.—CALCULATION OF PREMIUM

Diminution in the value of the landlord's interest—assumptions

(b) In *Grosvenor West End Properties v Whiston Properties Ltd* [2002] 2   **33–03**
E.G.L.R. 87, the Lands Tribunal held that the assumption of no 1993
Act rights applied when valuing the amount payable to the intermediate
landlord, as well as to the freeholder. The right to a new lease had to be
ignored in calculating the amount to be received by the headlessee
under a formula in the headlease.

In *Cadogan v Sportelli* [2007] 1 E.G.L.R. 153, the Lands Tribunal held that this
assumption precluded any allowance for "hope value" in the diminution of the
value of the landlord's interest: see paras 98–108. The hope value being referred
to is the prospect of the landlord granting a new lease to the tenant outside the
Act at some time before the existing lease expires. The Court of Appeal dismissed an appeal against the Lands Tribunal's decision on hope value: [2007]
EWCA Civ 1042. A petition for leave to appeal to the House of Lords is
expected.

Yield rates   **33–04**
In *Cadogan v Sportelli* [2007] 1 E.G.L.R. 153, the Lands Tribunal held that the
deferment rate for flats should be five per cent regardless of location. The effect
of a flat's location is reflected in the vacant possession values used in the
valuation. The decision was reached having considered that market evidence of
sales of reversions was tainted by the effect of rights under the Act and taking
account of a large amount of non-property financial evidence. The Lands Tribunal intended to give guidance which should be followed by tribunals in the
future, in order to avoid costly disputes as to the deferment rate to be used. The
Court of Appeal has dismissed the appeals against the Lands Tribunal's decision
on deferment rate: [2007] EWCA Civ 1042. This is effectively binding guidance
for properties within the Prime Central London area. Outside that area, it remains
open to valuers to seek to argue for a different rate, using five per cent as the
starting point: *per* Carnwath L.J. at para. 102.

The rate used to capitalise the freeholder's rental income should usually be considered separately from the deferment rate: *Nicholson v Goff* [2007] 1 E.G.L.R. 83, where at para. 9 the Lands Tribunal listed the factors which would influence that rate. These were (i) the length of the lease term; (ii) the security of recovery; (iii) the size of the ground rent (a larger ground rent being more attractive); (iv) whether there was provision for review of the ground rent; and (v) if there were such provision, the nature of it.

Marriage value

33–05   In *Chelsea Properties v Earl Cadogan and Cadogan Estates Ltd* [2007] PLSCS 197 the Lands Tribunal held that any "hope value" (the value representing the possibility of a deal being done between the landlord and the tenant) should also be disregarded when valuing the tenant's existing lease; see paragraph 19.

33–09   *Intermediate leases*

The issue as to the correct valuation of an intermediate leasehold interest in the flat in respect of which a new lease is being acquired has been the subject of a number of further cases, producing inconsistent results from leasehold valuation tribunals. The disputes largely concern whether the minor intermediate lease formula should be applied to value the intermediate lessee's interest after the grant of the new lease and, if not, the correct way of valuing the intermediate lessee's interest. At present, at least five appeals to the Lands Tribunal are pending, and it is anticipated that one or more of these appeals will provide much needed guidance.

Marriage value

Share of marriage value

33–11   At the bottom of p. 541 the last heading should read "Freeholder's proposed interest" instead of "Freeholder's present interest". At the top of p. 542, under "Calculation of marriage value", £144 being the value of the landlord's proposed interest should be added to the £200,000 in the top line of marriage value.

33–12   Under the Underlease details the fifth item should read "Rent receivable by headlessee" not "Rent received by headlease".

CHAPTER 34

MISCELLANEOUS

1.—MISSING LANDLORD—COLLECTIVE ENFRANCHISEMENT

Footnote 13: Now in paragraph 6.4.2 of the Land Registry Practice Guide 27 **34–03**
(November 2006).

Vesting Order
Add at end: In *R. (on the application of Ford (t/a David Sayers)) v Leasehold* **34–05**
Valuation Tribunal [2005] P.L.S.C.S. 43, Collins J. held that the tribunal has a
discretion under s. 27 of the 1993 Act to go behind a vesting order made by a
county court under s. 26 of the Act. The Tribunal ought not to have acceded to
the tenant's application that a garage, which had been converted by the (formerly
missing) landlord into a flat for his own use, was included in the collective
enfranchisement claim and should be valued as a garage. There was a significant
doubt about the status of the garage, and the tribunal should have made inquiries
to ascertain the true position to ensure that injustice was not done to the missing
landlord. The tribunal should have contacted the Land Registry to try to resolve
the obvious conflict between the relevant lease of the flat which allegedly
included the disputed garage and the freehold. The tribunal's decision was
quashed on the landlord's application for judicial review, and the matter remitted
for reconsideration.

Footnote 28: Now in paragraph 6.4.2 of the Land Registry Practice Guide 27 **34–06**
(November 2006).

2.—MISSING LANDLORD—NEW LEASE

Footnote 39: Now in paragraph 6.4.2 of the Land Registry Practice Guide 27 **34–08**
(November 2006).

Vesting order
Footnote 50: Now in paragraph 6.4.2 of the Land Registry Practice Guide 27 **34–10**
(November 2006).

3.—Special Categories of Landlord

(7) The Crown
34–15 The cross-reference should be to paragraph 14–46. The most recent form of undertaking is set out in paragraph 14–46 of this Supplement.

(8) National Trust
As under the 1967 Act, the property must be vested inalienably in the National Trust for the prohibition to apply.

4.—Other Matters

Notices
34–16 The fact that a notice may be sent by post brings into operation section 7 of the Interpretation Act 1978.

In *Glen International Ltd v Triplerose Ltd* [2007] EWCA Civ 388; [2007] 26 E.G. 164, the tenant served a s. 42 notice on the landlord's address sent out in the last rent demand, and relied on s. 47 of the Landlord and Tenant Act 1987. The landlord, who had not served a counter-notice, claimed to have served the tenant with an address for service under s. 48 of the 1987 Act, which accordingly superseded the rent demand address. The landlord's argument failed—the address had been supplied to a solicitor acting for the tenant on a different matter and did not constitute notice under s. 48. Moreover, the solicitor was not authorised to receive notice on behalf of the tenant under s. 48 of the 1987 Act.

Add:

Service on dead landlord

If the landlord is dead, a notice, *e.g.* a section 13 or section 42 notice, is sufficiently served before a grant of representation has been filed if it is addressed to "The Personal Representatives of" the deceased (naming him) and left at or sent by post to his last known place of residence or business in the United Kingdom, and a copy of it, similarly addressed, is served on the Public Trustee: s. 18(1) of the Law of Property (Miscellaneous Provisions) Act 1994. By s. 18(2), the filing of a grant of representation means the filing at the Principal Registry of the Family Division of the High Court of a copy of a grant of representation in respect of the deceased's estate or, as the case may be, the part of his estate which includes the land in question.

CHAPTER 35

1993 ACT PROCEEDINGS

2.—LEASEHOLD VALUATION TRIBUNAL

Footnote 9 should read s. 173(1) and (2), not s. 175(1) and (2).   **35–02**

In *Stephenson v Leathbond Ltd* [2005] 3 E.G.L.R. 79, it was held by the Lands Tribunal that the leasehold valuation tribunal, rather than the county court, had jurisdiction to decide whether a piece of land could be acquired as part of a collective enfranchisement claim. The issue was one of the 'terms of acquisition'. The landlord admitted that the participating tenants had the right to acquire the specified premises, the block of flats. There was a dispute about the tenants' claim to acquire an adjoining playground. The landlord's argument that the County Court had to determine that issue on an application to amend the initial notice under paragraph 15(2) of Schedule 3 to the 1993 Act was rejected.

Chapter 36

MANAGEMENT SCHEMES

3.—1993 Act Schemes

Other contents of scheme

The cases in Footnotes 90 and 91 were followed in *The Dulwich Estate v Baptiste*   **36–25**
[2007] 08 E.G. 137 (CS). An arbitrator had determined that the Estate was
unreasonable in refusing consent to a loft conversion; an appeal from his decision
was allowed. The test was whether the Estate's decision was within a general
band of reasonableness, not whether in the arbitrator's opinion consent should
have been given.

Charges under estate management schemes

In *Walker v Hampstead Garden Suburb Trust Ltd* (unreported, 2007), the LVT   **36–36**
held that it had no jurisdiction under s. 159(3) of the 2002 Act to vary a scheme.
The scheme required each owner to pay a management charge, being calculated
by dividing the annual (variable) expenditure by the number of enfranchised
properties. The applicant sought to vary the charge by linking the charge to the
value of each property. The tribunal held that the charge was a "variable estate
charge" within the meaning of s. 159(2), and thus the method of calculation
could not be varied under s. 159(3). The "formula" contemplated by both s.
159(2) and s. 159(3) is a formula which enables the estate charge to be calculated
without reference to the fluctuation of actual costs. Permission to appeal has been
granted to the applicant.

    Footnote 170: The commencement date for Wales is March 31, 2004. The
Order is set out at Appendix 2S.

PRECEDENTS

LEASEHOLD REFORM, HOUSING AND URBAN DEVELOPMENT ACT 1993

E. Collective Enfranchisement

PRECEDENT E16

Leasehold Reform, Housing and Urban Development Act 1993 Section 21

Counter-notice admitting claim

Replace paragraph 1 with the following text:

653 1. TAKE NOTICE that CD [the reversioner] admits that the participating tenants were on the relevant date entitled to exercise the right to collective enfranchisement in relation to the specified premises.

PRECEDENT E17

Leasehold Reform, Housing and Urban Development Act 1993 Section 21

Counter-notice not admitting claim

Replace paragraph 1 with the following text:

655 1. TAKE NOTICE that CD [the reversioner] does not admit that the participating tenants were on the relevant date entitled to exercise the right to collective enfranchisement in relation to the specified premises.

F. New Lease

PRECEDENT F3

Leasehold Reform, Housing and Urban Development Act 1993

Section 41(3)(c)

Notice

Replace heading with the following:

663   Leasehold Reform, Housing and Urban Development Act 1993

Section 41(3)(b)

APPENDICES

Contents

Add the following listings:

STATUTES

APPENDIX 1A

Leasehold Reform Act 1967

Tenants entitled to enfranchisement or extension

Replace section 1(1ZC)(c) with the following text: **683**

  (c) it is a tenancy taking effect under section 149(6) of the Law of Property Act 1925 (c.20) (leases terminable after a death or marriage [or the formation of a civil partnership],[8A] or

Add new Footnote 8A: Words inserted by Civil Partnership Act 2004, s. 81, Sch. 8, para. 3.

Replace sections 1(6) and 7 with the following text: **685**

  (6) If, in relation to any house and premises,—

    (a) the appropriate day for the purposes of subsection (1)(a) above falls before 1st April 1973, and

(b) the rateable value of the house and premises on the appropriate day was more than £200 or, if it was then in Greater London, £400, and

(c) the tenancy was created on or before 18th February 1966,

subsection (1)(a) above shall have effect in relation to the house and premises as if for the reference to the appropriate day there were substituted a reference to 1st April 1973 and as if for the sums of £200 and £400 specified in that subsection there were substituted respectively the sums of £750 and £1,500.[21]

[(7) The Secretary of State may by order replace the amount referred to in subsection (1)(a)(ii) above and the number in the definition of "I" in that subsection by such amount or number as is specified in the order; and such an order shall be made by statutory instrument which shall be subject to annulment in pursuance of a resolution of either House of Parliament.][22]

Replace Footnote 21 with the following: s. 1(5)(6) added by Housing Act (1974 c.44), s. 118(1)(5).
Replace Footnote 22 with the following: s. 1(7) added by SI 1990/434, reg. 2, Sch., para. 6.

Meaning of "long tenancy"

688–689   Replace section 3(1) with the following text:

   3.—(1) In this Part of this Act "long tenancy" means, subject to the provisions of this section, a tenancy granted for a term of years certain exceeding twenty-one years, whether or not the tenancy is (or may become) terminable before the end of that term by notice given by or to the tenant or by re-entry, forfeiture or otherwise, and includes [both a tenancy taking effect under section 149(6) of the Law of Property Act 1925 (leases terminable after a death or marriage [or the formation of a civil partnership][35A]) and][36] a tenancy for a term fixed by law under a grant with a covenant or obligation for perpetual renewal unless it is a tenancy by sub-demise from one which is not a long tenancy:

   [Provided that a tenancy granted so as to become terminable by notice after [a death, a marriage or the formation of a civil partnership][36A] is not to be treated as a long tenancy if—

   (a) the notice is capable of being given at any time after the death or marriage of [, or the formation of a civil partnership by,][36B] the tenant;

   (b) the length of the notice is not more than three months; and

   (c) the terms of the tenancy preclude both—

      (i) its assignment otherwise than by virtue of section 92 of the Housing Act 1985 (assignments by way of exchange), and

      (ii) the sub-letting of the whole of the premises comprised in it.][37]

Add new Footnote 35A: Inserted by Civil Partnership Act 2004, s. 81, Sch. 8, para. 5.
Replace Footnote 36 with the following: Words inserted by Leasehold Reform, Housing and Urban Development Act (1993 c.28), Pt I, c. III, s. 64(2)(a).
Add new Footnote 36A: Inserted by Civil Partnership Act 2004, s. 81, Sch. 8, para. 5.
Add new Footnote 36B: Inserted by Civil Partnership Act 2004, s. 81, Sch. 8, para. 5.
Replace Footnote 37 with the following: Words substituted by the Leasehold Reform, Housing and Urban Development Act (1993 c.28), Pt I, c.III, s. 64(2)(b).

Meaning of "low rent"

Replace section 4(1)(ii) with the following text: **690**

[(ii) if the tenancy [does not fall within paragraph (i) above,][44] more than £1,000 if the property is in Greater London and £250 if the property is elsewhere.[44A]

Replace Footnote 44 with the following: Words substituted by Housing Act (1996 c.52), Pt III, c.III, s. 105(1)(b).
Add new Footnote 44A: Inserted by SI 1990/34, reg. 2, Sch., para. 7(b).

General provisions as to claims to enfranchisement or extension

Replace section 5(5) with the following text: **694**

(5) No lease shall be registrable under [the Land Charges Act 1972][51] or be deemed to be an estate contract within the meaning of that Act by reason of the rights conferred on the tenant by this Part of this Act to acquire the freehold or an extended lease of property thereby demised, nor shall any right of a tenant arising from a notice under this Act of his desire to have the freehold or to have an extended lease be [regarded for the purposes of the Land Registration Act 2002 as an interest falling within any of the paragraphs of Schedule 1 or 3 to that Act];[51A] but any such notice shall be registrable under [the Land Charges Act 1972][52] or may be the subject of a notice [under the Land Registration Act 2002],[52A] as if it were an estate contract.

Replace Footnote 51 with the following: Words substituted by virtue of Land Charges Act (1972 c.61), s. 18(6).
Replace Footnote 51A with the following: Words substituted by virtue of Land Registration Act (2002 c.9), Sch. 11, para. 8(2).
Replace Footnote 52 with the following: Words substituted by virtue of Land Charges Act (1972 c.61), s. 18(6).
Replace Footnote 52A with the following: Words substituted by virtue of Land Registration Act (2002 c.9), Sch. 11, para. 8(2).

Rights of trustees

Replace section 6(5) with the following text: **696**

(5) The purposes authorised for the application of capital money by section 73 of the Settled Land Act 1925 [. . .][57] and the purposes authorised by section 71 of the Settled Land Act 1925 as purposes for which moneys may be raised by mortgage, shall include the payment of any expenses incurred by a tenant for life [. . .][58] in or in connection with proceedings taken by him [. . .][59] by virtue of subsection (2) or (3) above.

Replace Footnote 57 with the following: Words repealed by Trusts of Land and Appointment of Trustees Act (1996 c.47), Sch. 4, para. 1.
Replace Footnote 58 with the following: Words repealed by Commonhold and Leasehold Reform Act (2002 c.15), s. 180, Sch. 14.
Replace Footnote 59 with the following: Words repealed by Commonhold and Leasehold Reform Act (2002 c.15), s. 180, Sch. 14.

Rights of members of family succeeding to tenancy on death

Replace section 7(7) and (8) with the following text: **697**

(7) For purposes of this section a person is a member of another's family if that person is—

(a) the other's [spouse or civil partner];[69A] or

(b) a son or daughter or a son-in-law or daughter-in-law of the other, or of the other's [spouse or civil partner];[69B] or

(c) the father or mother of the other, or of the other's [spouse or civil partner][69C].

In paragraph (b) above any reference to a person's son or daughter includes a reference to any stepson or stepdaughter, any illegitimate son or daughter, [...][70] of that person, and "son-in-law" and "daughter-in-law" shall be construed accordingly.

(8) In Schedule 2 to the Intestates' Estates Act 1952 (which gives a surviving spouse a right to require the deceased's interest in the matrimonial home to be appropriated to the survivor's interest in the deceased's estate, but by paragraph 1(2) excludes tenancies terminating, or terminable by the landlord, within two years of the death), paragraph 1(2) shall not apply to a tenancy if—

(a) the surviving [spouse or civil partner][70A] would in consequence of an appropriation in accordance with that paragraph become entitled by virtue of this section to acquire the freehold or an extended lease under this Part of this Act, either immediately on the appropriation or before the tenancy can determine or be determined as mentioned in paragraph 1(2); or

(b) the deceased [spouse or civil partner],[70B] being entitled to acquire the freehold or an extended lease under this Part of this Act, had given notice of his or her desire to have it and the benefit of that notice is appropriated with the tenancy.

Add new Footnote 69A: Substituted by Civil Partnership Act 2004, s. 81, Sch. 8, para. 6.
Add new Footnote 69B: Substituted by Civil Partnership Act 2004, s. 81, Sch. 8, para. 6.
Add new Footnote 69C: Substituted by Civil Partnership Act 2004, s. 81, Sch. 8, para. 6.
Footnote 70: Words repealed by Children Act (1975 c.72), Sch. 4 Pt. I.
Add new Footnote 70A: Substituted by Civil Partnership Act 2004, s. 81, Sch. 8, para. 6.
Add new Footnote 70B: Substituted by Civil Partnership Act 2004, s. 81, Sch. 8, para. 6.

Purchase price and costs of enfranchisement, and tenant's right to withdraw
704   9.—

Add to Footnote 90: Date in force (in relation to Wales): March 30, 2004, see SI 2004/669.

Rights to be conveyed to tenant on enfranchisement
705   10.—

Replace Footnote 95 with the following: Words inserted by Law of Property (Miscellaneous Provisions) Act (1994 c.36) Sch. 1, para. 5(1).

Obligation to grant extended lease
713   14.—

Add to Footnote 102: Date in force (in relation to Wales): March 30, 2004, see SI 2004/669.

Residential rights (exclusion of enfranchisement or extension)
Replace section 18(3) with the following text: **720**

(3) Where the landlord's interest is held on trust, subsection (1) above shall apply as if the reference to occupation as the residence of the landlord were a reference to the like occupation of a person having an interest under the trust (whether or not also a trustee), and the reference to a member of the landlord's family were a reference to the like member of such a person's family; and for purposes of subsection (1) a person is an adult member of another's family if that person is—

(a) the other's [spouse or civil partner];[116A] or
(b) a son or daughter or a son-in-law or daughter-in-law of the other, or of the other's [spouse or civil partner],[116B] who has attained the age of eighteen; or
(c) the father or mother of the other, or of the other's [spouse or civil partner].[116C]

In paragraph (b) above any reference to a person's son or daughter includes a reference to any stepson or stepdaughter, any illegitimate son or daughter, [. . .][117] of that person, and "son-in-law" and "daughter-in-law" shall be construed accordingly.

Add new Footnote 116A: Substituted by Civil Partnership Act 2004, s. 81, Sch. 8, para. 7.
Add new Footnote 116B: Substituted by Civil Partnership Act 2004, s. 81, Sch. 8, para. 7.
Add new Footnote 116C: Substituted by Civil Partnership Act 2004, s. 81, Sch. 8, para. 7.
Footnote 117: Words repealed by Children Act (1975 c.72), Sch. 4, Pt. I.

Jurisdiction and special powers of county court
  20.—   **727**

Add to Footnote 120: Date in force (in relation to Wales): March 30, 2004, see SI 2004/669.

Jurisdiction of Lands Tribunal
Replace section 21(1) with the following: **728–730**
  21.—(1) The following matters shall, in default of agreement, be determined by [a leasehold valuation tribunal][121] namely,—

(a)   the price payable for a house and premises under section 9 above;
(b)   the amount of the rent to be payable (whether originally or on a revision) for a house and premises in accordance with section 15(2);
[(ba)   the amount of any costs payable under section 9(4) or 14(2);][122]
(c)   the amount of any compensation payable to a tenant under section 17 or 18 for the loss of a house and premises.
[(cza) the amount of the appropriate sum to be paid into court under section 27(5);][123]
[(ca)   the amount of any compensation payable under section 27A;[124]
[[. . .][125]

Replace Footnote 121 with the following: Words substituted by Housing Act (1980 c.51), Sch. 22, para. 8(1).
Replace Footnote 122 with the following: Added by Housing Act (1996 c.52), Pt III, c.III, s. 115.
Replace Footnote 123 with the following: Subs. (1)(cza) added by Commonhold and Leasehold Reform Act (2002 c.15), s. 149(2). Date in force (in relation to England only): September 30, 2003, see SI 2003/1986. Date in force (in relation to Wales): March 30, 2004, see SI 2004/669.
Replace Footnote 124 with the following: Added by Housing Act (1996 c.52) Sch. 11, para. 1(2).
Replace Footnote 125 with the following: Subs.(1A) repealed by Commonhold and Leasehold Reform Act (2002 c.15), s. 180, Sch. 14. Date in force (in relation to England only): September 30, 2003, see SI 2003/1986. Date in force (in relation to Wales): March 30, 2004, see SI 2004/669.
Add to Footnote 129: Date in force (in relation to Wales): March 30, 2004, see SI 2004/669.

Replace sections 21(3), (4) and (4A) with the following:

(3) [...][130]

(4) [...][131]

(4A) [...][132]

Replace Footnote 130 with the following: Repealed by Commonhold and Leasehold Reform Act (2002 c.15), s. 180, Sch. 14. Date in force (in relation to England only): September 30, 2003, see SI 2003/1986. Date in force (in relation to Wales): March 30, 2004, see SI 2004/669.
Replace Footnote 131 with the following: Repealed by Commonhold and Leasehold Reform Act (2002 c.15), s. 180, Sch. 14. Date in force (in relation to England only): September 30, 2003, see SI 2003/1986. Date in force (in relation to Wales): March 30, 2004, see SI 2004/669.
Replace Footnote 132 with the following: Repealed by Commonhold and Leasehold Reform Act (2002 c.15), s. 180, Sch. 14. Date in force (in relation to England only): September 30, 2003, see SI 2003/1986. Date in force (in relation to Wales): March 30, 2004, see SI 2004/669.

Delete Footnotes 133–136.

Validity of tenant's notices, effect on Landlord and Tenant Act 1954 and on notices to quit etc., and procedure generally

22.—

Replace section 22(2) with the following:

(2) Where a tenant having a right under this Part of this Act to acquire the freehold or an extended lease gives the landlord notice in accordance with this Part of this Act of his desire to have it, then except as otherwise provided by this Act the procedure for giving effect to the notice, and the rights and obligations of all parties in relation to the investigation of title and other matters arising in giving effect to the notice, shall be such as may be prescribed by regulations made by [the Secretary of State][138A] by statutory instrument (which shall be subject to annulment in pursuance of a resolution of either House of Parliament), and subject to or in the absence of provision made by any such regulations as regards any matter shall be as nearly as may be the same as in the case of a contract of sale or leasing freely negotiated between the parties.

Add new Footnote 138A: Words substituted by SI 1974/1896, art. 3(2).

Person to act where landlord is custodian trustee or under disability

735   26.—

Replace section 26(2) with the following:

(2) Where a landlord is incapable by reason of mental disorder within the meaning of the [Mental Health Act 1983][145] of managing and administering his

property and affairs, his receiver [appointed under Part VII of the said Act of 1983 or Part VIII of the Mental Health Act 1959][146] or (if no such receiver is acting for him) any person authorised in that behalf shall, under an order of the authority [having jurisdiction under Part VII of the said Act of 1983],[147] take his place as landlord for purposes of this Part of this Act.

Replace Footnote 145 with the following: Words substituted by Mental Health Act (1983 c.20), s. 148, Sch. 4, para. 22.
Replace Footnote 146 with the following: Words substituted by Mental Health Act (1983 c.20), s. 148, Sch. 4, para. 22.
Replace Footnote 147 with the following: Words substituted by Mental Health Act (1983 c.20), s. 148, Sch. 4, para. 22.

Enfranchisement where landlord cannot be found
Replace section 27 with the following: **735–737**

27.—(1) Where a tenant of a house having a right under this Part of this Act to acquire the freehold is prevented from giving notice of his desire to have the freehold because the person to be served with the notice cannot be found, or his identity cannot be ascertained, then on an application made by the tenant [the court][148] may, subject to and in accordance with the provisions of this section, make such order as [the court][149] thinks fit with a view to the house and premises being vested in him, his executors, administrators or assigns for the like estate and on the like terms (so far as the circumstances permit) as if he had at the date of his application to [the court][150] given notice of his desire to have the freehold.

(2) Before making any such order [the court][151] may require the applicant to take such further steps by way of advertisement or otherwise as [the court][152] thinks proper for the purpose of tracing the landlord; and if after an application is made to [the court][153] and before the house and premises are vested in pursuance of the application the landlord is traced, then no further proceedings shall be taken with a view to the house and premises being so vested, but subject to subsection (7) below—

(a) the rights and obligations of all parties shall be determined as if the applicant had, at the date of the application, duly given notice of his desire to have the freehold; and

(b) [the court][154] may give such directions as [the court][155] thinks fit as to the steps to be taken for giving effect to those rights and obligations, including directions modifying or dispensing with any of the requirements of this Act or of regulations made under this Act.

(3) Where a house and premises are to be vested in a person in pursuance of an application under this section, then on his paying into [court][156] the appropriate sum there shall be executed by such person as the [court][157] may designate a conveyance in a form approved by the [court][158] and containing such provisions as may be so approved for the purpose of giving effect so far as possible to the requirements of section 10 above; and that conveyance shall be effective to vest in the person to whom the conveyance is made the property expressed to be

conveyed, subject as and in the manner in which it is expressed to be conveyed.

(4) For the purpose of any conveyance to be executed in accordance with subsection (3) above, any question as to the property to be conveyed and the rights with or subject to which it is to be conveyed shall be determined by the [court],[159] but it shall be assumed (unless the contrary is shown) that the landlord has no interest in property other than the property to be conveyed and, for the purpose of excepting them from the conveyance, any underlying minerals.

[(5) The appropriate sum which, in accordance with subsection (3) above, is to be paid into court is the aggregate of—

    (a) such amount as may be determined by (or on appeal from) a leasehold valuation tribunal to be the price payable in accordance with section 9 above; and

    (b) the amount or estimated amount (as so determined) of any pecuniary rent payable for the house and premises up to the date of the conveyance which remains unpaid.][160]

(6) Where a house and premises are vested in a person in accordance with this section, the payment into [court][161] of the appropriate sum shall be taken to have satisfied any claims against the tenant, his executors, administrators or assigns in respect of the price payable under this Part of this Act for the acquisition of the freehold in the house and premises.

(7) An application under this section may be withdrawn at any time before execution of a conveyance under subsection (3) above and, after it is withdrawn, subsection (2)(a) shall not apply; but where any step is taken (whether by the landlord or the tenant) for the purpose of giving effect to subsection (2)(a) in the case of any application, the application shall not afterwards be withdrawn except with the landlord's consent or by leave of [the court],[162] and [the court][163] shall not give leave unless it appears to [the court][164] just to do so by reason of matters coming to the knowledge of the applicant in consequence of the landlord being traced.

(8) A conveyance executed under subsection (3) above shall have effect as provided by that subsection notwithstanding any interest of the Crown in the property expressed to be conveyed.

Replace Footnote 148 with the following: Words substituted by Commonhold and Leasehold Reform Act (2002 c.15), s. 148(2)(a). Date in force (in relation to England only): September 30, 2003, see SI 2003/1986. Date in force (in relation to Wales): March 30, 2004, see SI 2004/669.
Replace Footnote 149 with the following: Words substituted by Commonhold and Leasehold Reform Act (2002 c.15), s. 148(2)(b). Date in force (in relation to England only): September 30, 2003, see SI 2003/1986. Date in force (in relation to Wales): March 30, 2004, see SI 2004/669.
Replace Footnote 150 with the following: Words substituted by Commonhold and Leasehold Reform Act (2002 c.15), s. 148(2)(a). Date in force (in relation to England only): September 30, 2003, see SI 2003/1986. Date in force (in relation to Wales): March 30, 2004, see SI 2004/669.
Replace Footnote 151 with the following: Words substituted by Commonhold and Leasehold Reform Act (2002 c.15), s. 148(3)(a). Date in force (in relation to England only): September 30, 2003, see SI 2003/1986. Date in force (in relation to Wales): March 30, 2004, see SI 2004/669.
Replace Footnote 152 with the following: Words substituted by Commonhold and Leasehold Reform Act (2002 c.15), s. 148(3)(b). Date in force (in relation to England only): September 30, 2003, see SI 2003/1986. Date in force (in relation to Wales): March 30, 2004, see SI 2004/669.

Replace Footnote 153 with the following: Words substituted by Commonhold and Leasehold Reform Act (2002 c.15), s. 148(3)(a). Date in force (in relation to England only): September 30, 2003, see SI 2003/1986. Date in force (in relation to Wales): March 30, 2004, see SI 2004/669.

Replace Footnote 154 with the following: Words substituted by Commonhold and Leasehold Reform Act (2002 c.15), s. 148(3)(a). Date in force (in relation to England only): September 30, 2003, see SI 2003/1986. Date in force (in relation to Wales): March 30, 2004, see SI 2004/669.

Replace Footnote 155 with the following: Words substituted by Commonhold and Leasehold Reform Act (2002 c.15), s. 148(3)(b). Date in force (in relation to England only): September 30, 2003, see SI 2003/1986. Date in force (in relation to Wales): March 30, 2004, see SI 2004/669.

Replace Footnote 156 with the following: Word substituted by Commonhold and Leasehold Reform Act (2002 c.15), s. 148(4)(a). Date in force (in relation to England only): September 30, 2003, see SI 2003/1986. Date in force (in relation to Wales): March 30, 2004, see SI 2004/669.

Replace Footnote 157 with the following: Word substituted by Commonhold and Leasehold Reform Act (2002 c.15), s. 148(4)(b). Date in force (in relation to England only): September 30, 2003, see SI 2003/1986. Date in force (in relation to Wales): March 30, 2004, see SI 2004/669.

Replace Footnote 158 with the following: Word substituted by Commonhold and Leasehold Reform Act (2002 c.15), s. 148(4)(b). Date in force (in relation to England only): September 30, 2003, see SI 2003/1986. Date in force (in relation to Wales): March 30, 2004, see SI 2004/669.

Replace Footnote 159 with the following: Word substituted by Commonhold and Leasehold Reform Act (2002 c.15), s. 148(5). Date in force (in relation to England only): September 30, 2003, see SI 2003/1986. Date in force (in relation to Wales): March 30, 2004, see SI 2004/669.

Replace Footnote 160 with the following: Subs. (5) substituted by Commonhold and Leasehold Reform Act (2002 c.15), s. 149(1). Date in force (in relation to England only): September 30, 2003, see SI 2003/1986. Date in force (in relation to Wales): March 30, 2004, see SI 2004/669.

Replace Footnote 161 with the following: Word substituted by Commonhold and Leasehold Reform Act (2002 c.15), s. 148(6). Date in force (in relation to England only): September 30, 2003, see SI 2003/1986. Date in force (in relation to Wales): March 30, 2004, see SI 2004/669.

Replace Footnote 162 with the following: Words substituted by Commonhold and Leasehold Reform Act (2002 c.15), s. 148(7)(a). Date in force (in relation to England only): September 30, 2003, see SI 2003/1986. Date in force (in relation to Wales): March 30, 2004, see SI 2004/669.

Replace Footnote 163 with the following: Words substituted by Commonhold and Leasehold Reform Act (2002 c.15), s. 148(7)(a). Date in force (in relation to England only): September 30, 2003, see SI 2003/1986. Date in force (in relation to Wales): March 30, 2004, see SI 2004/669.

Replace Footnote 164 with the following: Words substituted by Commonhold and Leasehold Reform Act (2002 c.15), s. 148(7)(b). Date in force (in relation to England only): September 30, 2003, see SI 2003/1986. Date in force (in relation to Wales): March 30, 2004, see SI 2004/669.

Retention or resumption of land required for public purposes
28.—   742

Section 28(5)(bc) was repealed by the Serious Organised Crime and Police Act 2005, ss. 59, 174, Sch. 4, para. 17 and Sch. 17 Pt 2.

Replace section 28(5)(d) with the following:

> [(d) to [any Strategic Health Authority],[182] any [[Health Authority, any Special Health Authority][183] [, any Primary Care Trust][184] [, any National Health Service trust and any NHS foundation trust]],[185] and][186]

Replace Footnote 182 with the following: Words inserted by SI 2002/2469 Sch. 1(1), para. 4(a).

Replace Footnote 183 with the following: Words substituted by Health Authorities Act (1995 c.17) Sch. 1(III), para. 94(a).

Replace Footnote 184 with the following: Words inserted by SI 2000/90 Sch. 1, para. 7(a).

Replace Footnote 185 with the following: Words substituted by Health and Social Care (Community Health and Standards) Act (2003 c.43), Sch. 4, para. 12.

Replace Footnote 186 with the following: s. 28(5)(d) substituted by National Health Service Reorganisation Act (1973 c.32), Sch. 4, para. 111(1).

743   Replace section 28(6)(b) with the following:

> (b) the treatment as a whole, by development, redevelopment, or improvement, or partly by one and partly by another method, of any area in which the property is situated.

744   Replace section 28(6)(c) with the following:

> [(c) to [any Strategic Health Authority],[182] any [[Health Authority, any Special Health Authority][183] [, any Primary Care Trust][184] [, any National Health Service trust and any NHS foundation trust]],[185] and][186]

Replace Footnote 194 with the following: Words inserted by SI 2002/2469, Sch. 1(1), para. 4(b).
Replace Footnote 195 with the following: Words substituted by Health Authorities Act (1995 c.17), Sch. 1(III), para. 94(b).
Replace Footnote 196 with the following: Words inserted by SI 2000/90, Sch. 1, para. 7(b).
Replace Footnote 197 with the following: Words substituted by Health and Social Care (Community Health and Standards) Act (2003 c.43), Sch. 4, para. 12.
Replace Footnote 198 with the following: Substituted by the National Health Service (Sonsequential Provisions) Act 2006, s. 2, Sch. 1, para. 22.
Replace Footnote 199 with the following: s. 28(6)(c) substituted by National Health Service Reorganisation Act (1973 c.32), Sch. 4, para. 111(2).

Reservation of future right to develop
745   In s. 29(6), the words from "but a university body" to the end were repealed by s. 177(2) of the Education and Inspections Act 2006.

By s. 177(3) of the Act, in s. 29(6B), for the words from "includes" to the end, substitute:

> "(a) includes development by a related university body (within the meaning of section 28(6)(b) above); and
> (b) must be development for the purposes (other than investment purposes) of the university body or any such related university body."

766   **8.—**

Add to Footnote 263: Date in force (in relation to Wales): March 30, 2004, see SI 2004/669.

Replace paragraph 9(1) of Schedule 2 with the following:
9.—(1) The purposes authorised for the application of capital money by section 73 of the Settled Land Act 1925 [. . .][264A] and the purposes authorised by section 71 of the Settled Land Act 1925 [. . .][264B] as purposes for which moneys may be raised by mortgage, shall include the payment of compensation in accordance with section 17 or 18 of this Act (whether possession is obtained under that section or without any application for possession).

Add Footnote 264A: Words repealed by Trusts of Land and Appointment of Trustees Act (1996 c.47), Sch. 4.

Add Footnote 264B: Words repealed by Trusts of Land and Appointment of Trustees Act (1996 c.47), Sch. 4.

Replace paragraph 2(1) of Schedule 3 with the following:

2.—[(1) Sub-paragraphs (1A) to (1E) below apply where a landlord's notice **767** terminating the tenancy of any property has been given under section 4 or 25 of the Landlord and Tenant Act 1954 or served under paragraph 4(1) of Schedule 10 to the Local Government and Housing Act 1989 (whether or not that notice has effect to terminate the tenancy).

(1A) A claim to acquire the freehold or an extended lease of the property shall be of no effect if made after the relevant time, but this sub-paragraph is subject to sub-paragraphs (1D) and (1E) below.

(1B) In this paragraph (but subject to sub-paragraph (1C) below) "the relevant time" is the end of the period of two months beginning with the date on which the landlord's notice terminating the tenancy has been given or served.

(1C) Where—

(a) a landlord's notice terminating the tenancy has been given under section 25 of the Landlord and Tenant Act 1954, and
(b) the tenant applies to the court under section 24(1) of that Act for an order for the grant of a new tenancy before the end of the period of two months mentioned in sub-paragraph (1B) above,

"the relevant time" is the time when the application is made.

(1D) Sub-paragraph (1A) above shall not apply where the landlord gives his written consent to the claim being made after the relevant time.

(1E) Where a tenant, having given notice of a desire to have the freehold, gives after the relevant time a further notice under section 9(3) of this Act of his inability or unwillingness to acquire the house and premises at the price he must pay, he may with the notice under section 9(3) give a notice of his desire to have an extended lease (if he then has a right to such a lease).][266]

Replace Footnote 266 with the following: Subsection (1) substituted and (1A)–(1E) inserted by SI 2003/3096, Sch. 5, para. 11.

Replace paragraph 2(4) of Schedule 3 with the following:

(4) Where by virtue of sub-paragraph (3) above a landlord's notice specifies as the date of termination of a tenancy a date earlier than six months after the giving of the notice, then—

(a) if it is a notice proposing a statutory tenancy, section 7(2) of the Landlord and Tenant Act 1954 shall apply in relation to the notice with the substitution, for references to the period of two months ending with the date of termination specified in the notice and the beginning of that period, of references to the period of three months beginning with the giving of the notice and the end of that period [. . .][272A]
(b) [. . .][272B]

[2A—(1) If—

    (a) the landlord commences proceedings under Part 2 of the Landlord and Tenant Act 1954; and

    (b) the tenant subsequently makes a claim to acquire the freehold or an extended lease of the property; and

    (c) paragraph 2 above does not render the claim of no effect,

no further steps shall be taken in the proceedings under Part 2 otherwise than for their dismissal and for the making of any consequential order.

(2) Section 64 of the Landlord and Tenant Act 1954 shall have no effect in a case to which sub-paragraph (1) above applies.][272C]

Add new Footnote 272A: Word repealed by SI 2003/3096, Sch. 6.
Add new Footnote 272B: Repealed by SI 2003/3096, Sch. 6.
Add new Footnote 272C: Inserted by SI 2003/3096, Sch. 5, para. 12.

772   Insert paragraph 10(2A) of Schedule 3 as follows:

[(2A) If the landlord's notice is under section 25 of the Landlord and Tenant Act 1954, sub-paragraph (2) above shall effect in relation to it as if in paragraph (b), after the word "operate" there were inserted the words "and no further proceedings may be taken by him under Part 2 of the Landlord and Tenant Act 1954."][284A]

Add new Footnote 284A: Inserted by SI 2003/3096, Sch. 5, para. 13.

773   Replace paragraph 1(3) of Schedule 4 with the following:

    [(a) the covenant may be the subject of a notice in the register of title kept under the Land Registration Act 2002, if apart from this subsection it would not be capable of being the subject of such a notice; and][288A]

    (b) where [a notice in respect of the covenant has been entered in that register, it][288B] shall be binding upon every successor of the covenantor, if apart from this subsection it would not be binding upon every such successor.

Add new Footnote 288A: Words substituted by Land Registration Act (2002 c.9), Sch. 11, para. 8(3).
Add new Footnote 288B: Words substituted by Land Registration Act (2002 c.9), Sch. 11, para. 8(3).

APPENDIX 1B

Housing Act 1974

SCHEDULES

Replace paragraphs 1 and 2 of Schedule 8 with the following: **781–782**

1.—(1) Where the tenant, or any previous tenant, has made or contributed to the cost of an improvement on the premises comprised in the tenancy and the improvement is one to which this Schedule applies, then, if the tenant serves on the landlord a notice in the prescribed form requiring him to agree to a reduction under this Schedule, their rateable value as ascertained for the purposes of [section 1 of the Leasehold Reform Act 1967][316A] shall be reduced by such amount, if any, as may be agreed or determined in accordance with the following provisions of this Schedule.

(2) This Schedule applies to any improvement made by the execution of works amounting to structural alteration, extension or addition.

2.—(1) The amount of any such reduction may at any time be agreed in writing between the landlord and the tenant.

(2) Where, at the expiration of a period of six weeks from the service of a notice under paragraph 1 of this Schedule any of the following matters has not been agreed in writing between the landlord and the tenant, that is to say,—

(a) whether the improvement specified in the notice is an improvement to which this Schedule applies;
(b) what works were involved in it;
(c) whether the tenant or a previous tenant under the tenancy has made it or contributed to its cost; and
(d) what proportion his contribution, if any, bears to the whole cost the county court may on the application of the tenant determine that matter [. . .][316B]

(3) An application under the last foregoing sub-paragraph must be made within six weeks from the expiration of the period mentioned therein or such longer time as the court may allow.

Add new Footnote 316A: Words substituted by Housing Act 1980, s. 141, Sch. 21, para. 8(a).
Add new Footnote 316B: Words repealed by Housing Act 1980, ss. 141, 152, Sch. 21, para. 8(b).

Replace paragraph 3(2) of Schedule 8 with the following:
(2) On any such application the valuation officer shall certify—

(a) whether or not the improvement has affected the rateable value on the 1st April, 1973 (as ascertained for the purposes of [section 1 of the Leasehold Reform Act 1967][316C] of the hereditament of which the premises consist or, as the case may be, in which they are wholly or partly comprised, and
(b) if it has, the amount by which the rateable value would have been less if the improvement had not been made.

Add new Footnote 316C: Words substituted by Housing Act 1980, s. 141, Sch. 21, para. 8(c).

Replace paragraph 4 of Schedule 8 with the following:
[**4.**—Where a notice under paragraph 1 of this Schedule is served on or after 21st December 1979, the tenant shall bear the reasonable costs incurred by the landlord in investigating any matter specified in it.][316D]

Add new Footnote 316D: Paragraph inserted by Housing Act 1980, s. 141, Sch. 21, para. 8(c).

APPENDIX 1D

Housing Act 1980

Leasehold valuation tribunals
786–787 Replace section 142 with the following:
142.—(1) Any matter which under section 21(1), (2) or (3) of the Leasehold Reform Act 1967 is to be determined by the Lands Tribunal shall instead be determined by a [leasehold valuation tribunal][317]

(2) [...][318]

(3) [...][318A] The 1967 Act is amended in accordance with [Schedule 22 to this Act][319]

Replace Footnote 317 with the following: Words "leasehold valuation tribunal" substituted for "rent assessment committee constituted under Schedule 10 to the 1977 Act" in square brackets by Commonhold and Leasehold Reform Act (2002 c.15) s. 180, Sch. 13, para. 7(2). Date in force (in relation to England only): September 30, 2003, see SI 2003/1986. Date in force (in relation to Wales): March 30, 2004, see SI 2004/669.

Replace Footnote 318 with the following: Subs. (2) repealed by Commonhold and Leasehold Reform Act (2002 c.15), s. 180, Sch. 14. Date in force (in relation to England only): September 30, 2003, see SI 2003/1986. Date in force (in relation to Wales) March 30, 2004, see SI 2004/669.

Add new Footnote 318A: Words repealed by the Commonhold and Leasehold Reform Act (2002 c.15), s. 180, Sch. 14. Date in force (in relation to England only): September 30, 2003, see SI 2003/1986. Date in force (in relation to Wales): March 30, 2004, see SI 2004/669.

Replace Footnote 319 with the following: Words substituted by the Commonhold and Leasehold Reform Act (2002 c.15), s. 176, Sch. 13, para. 7(3). Date in force (in relation to England only): September 30, 2003, see SI 2003/1986. Date in force (in relation to Wales): March 30, 2004, see SI 2004/669.

Replace section 142(1) to (7) of Schedule 22 with the following:
1. [...][320]
2. [...][321]
3. [...][322]
4. [...][322A]
5. [...][322B]
6. [...][322C]
7. [...][322D]

Replace Footnote 320 with the following: Repealed by Commonhold and Leasehold Reform Act (2002 c.15), s. 180, Sch. 14. Date in force (in relation to England only): September 30, 2003, see SI 2003/1986. Date in force (in relation to Wales): March 30, 2004, see SI 2004/669.

Replace Footnote 321 with the following: Repealed by Commonhold and Leasehold Reform Act (2002 c.15), s. 180, Sch. 14. Date in force (in relation to England only): September 30, 2003, see SI 2003/1986. Date in force (in relation to Wales): March 30, 2004, see SI 2004/669.

Replace Footnote 322 with the following: Repealed by Commonhold and Leasehold Reform Act (2002 c.15), s. 180, Sch. 14. Date in force (in relation to England only): September 30, 2003, see SI 2003/1986. Date in force (in relation to Wales): March 30, 2004, see SI 2004/669.

Add new Footnote 322A: Repealed by Commonhold and Leasehold Reform Act (2002 c.15), s. 180, Sch. 14. Date in force (in relation to England only): September 30, 2003, see SI 2003/1986. Date in force (in relation to Wales): March 30, 2004, see SI 2004/669.

Add new Footnote 322B: Repealed by Commonhold and Leasehold Reform Act (2002 c.15), s. 180, Sch. 14. Date in force (in relation to England only): September 30, 2003, see SI 2003/1986. Date in force (in relation to Wales): March 30, 2004, see SI 2004/669.

Add new Footnote 322C: Repealed by Commonhold and Leasehold Reform Act (2002 c.15), s. 180, Sch. 14. Date in force (in relation to England only): September 30, 2003, see SI 2003/1986. Date in force (in relation to Wales): March 30, 2004, see SI 2004/669.

Add new Footnote 322D: Repealed by Commonhold and Leasehold Reform Act (2002 c.15), s. 180, Sch. 14. Date in force (in relation to England only): September 30, 2003, see SI 2003/1986. Date in force (in relation to Wales): March 30, 2004, see SI 2004/669.

APPENDIX 1G

Leasehold Reform, Housing and Urban Development Act 1993

Meaning of long lease

802–803 Replace section 7(1), (2) with the following text:
   7.—(1) In this Chapter "long lease" means (subject to the following provisions of this section)—

   (a) a lease granted for a term of years certain exceeding 21 years, whether or not it is (or may become) terminable before the end of that term by notice given by or to the tenant or by re-entry, forfeiture or otherwise;

   (b) a lease for a term fixed by law under a grant with a covenant or obligation for perpetual renewal (other than a lease by sub-demise from one which is not a long lease) or a lease taking effect under section 149(6) of the Law of Property Act 1925 (leases terminable after a death or marriage [or the formation of a civil partnership];)[355A]

   (c) a lease granted in pursuance of the right to buy conferred by Part V of the Housing Act 1985 or in pursuance of the right to acquire on rent to mortgage terms conferred by that Part of that Act; [. . .][356]

   (d) a shared ownership lease, whether granted in pursuance of that Part of that Act or otherwise, where the tenant's total share is 100 per cent [or][357]

   [(e) a lease granted in pursuance of that Part of that Act as it has effect by virtue of section 17 of the Housing Act 1996 (the right to acquire).][358]

   (2) A lease terminable by notice after [a death, a marriage or the formation of a civil partnership][358A] is not to be treated as a long lease for the purposes of this Chapter if—

   (a) the notice is capable of being given at any time after the death or marriage of [or the formation of a civil partnership by][358B] the tenant;

   (b) the length of the notice is not more than three months; and

   (c) the terms of the lease preclude both—
      (i) its assignment otherwise than by virtue of section 92 of the Housing Act 1985 (assignments by way of exchange), and
      (ii) the sub-letting of the whole of the premises comprised in it.

Add new Footnote 355A: Inserted by Civil Partnership Act 2004, s. 81, Sch. 8, para. 47.
Footnote 356: Word repealed by SI 1997/627, Sch. 1, para. 7.
Footnote 357: Word inserted by SI 1997/627, Sch. 1, para. 7.
Footnote 358: S.7(1)(e) inserted by SI 1997/627, Sch. 1, para. 7.
Add new Footnote 358A: Words substituted by Civil Partnership Act 2004, s. 81, Sch. 8, para. 47.
Add new Footnote 358B: Inserted by Civil Partnership Act 2004, s. 81, Sch. 8, para. 47.

Premises with a resident landlord

Replace section 10(5) with the following text: **806**

(5) For the purposes of this section a person is an adult member of another's family if that person is—

(a) the other's [spouse or civil partner];[372A] or

(b) a son or daughter or a son-in-law or daughter-in-law of the other, or of the other's [spouse or civil partner],[372B] who has attained the age of 18; or

(c) the father or mother of the other, or of the other's [spouse or civil partner];[372C]

and in paragraph (b) any reference to a person's son or daughter includes a reference to any stepson or stepdaughter of that person, and "son-in-law" and "daughter-in-law" shall be construed accordingly.

Add new Footnote 372A: Words substituted by Civil Partnership Act 2004, s. 81, Sch. 8, para. 48.
Add new Footnote 372B: Words substituted by Civil Partnership Act 2004, s. 81, Sch. 8, para. 48.
Add new Footnote 372C: Words substituted by Civil Partnership Act 2004, s. 81, Sch. 8, para. 48.

Duty of nominee purchaser to disclose existence of agreements affecting specified premises etc

Replace the first two lines of section 18(1) with the following: **822**

(1) If at any time during the beginning with the relevant date and ending with the [time when a binding contract is entered into in pursuance of the initial notice][403A]

Add new Footnote 403A: Words substituted by Commonhold and Leasehold Reform Act 2002, s. 126(2).

Conveyance to nominee purchaser

Replace section 34(10) with the following: **847**

(10) Any such conveyance shall in addition contain a statement that it is a conveyance executed for the purposes of this Chapter; and any such statement shall comply with such requirements as may be prescribed by [land registration rules under the Land Registration Act 2002][419A]

Add new Footnote 419A: Words substituted by Land Registration Act (2002 c.9), Sch. 11, para. 30.

Notice by qualifying tenant of claim to exercise right

Delete section 42(3A).   **857**

Terms on which new lease is to be granted

Replace section 57(11) with the following: **876**

(11) The new lease shall contain a statement that it is a lease granted under section 56; and any such statement shall comply with such requirements as may

be prescribed by [land registration rules under the Land Registration Act 2002][446A]

Add new Footnote 446A: Words substituted by Land Registration Act (2002 c.9), Sch. 11, para. 30.

Approval by leasehold valuation tribunal of estate management scheme

888   Replace section 70(6) with the following:

[(6) Where the application is to be considered in an oral hearing, the tribunal shall afford to any person making representations under subsection (4)(b) about the application an opportunity to appear at the hearing.][455]

Replace Footnote 455 with the following: Substituted by Commonhold and Leasehold Reform Act (2002 c.15), s. 176, Sch. 13, para. 12(2). Date in force (in relation to England only): September 30, 2003, see SI 2003/1986. Date in force (in relation to Wales): March 30, 2004, see SI 2004/669.

889   Replace section 70(10A) with the following:

[(10A) Any person who makes representations under subsection (4)(b) about an application for the approval of a scheme may appeal from a decision of the tribunal in proceedings on the application.][456]

Replace Footnote 456 with the following: Added by Commonhold and Leasehold Reform Act (2002 c.15), s. 176, Sch. 13, paragraph 13(3). Date in force (in relation to England only): September 30, 2003, see SI 2003/1986. Date in force (in relation to Wales): March 30, 2004, see SI 2004/669.

Variation of existing schemes

897   Replace section 75(4) and (5) with the following:

(4) [...][459A]
(5) [...][460]

Add new Footnote 459A: Repealed by Commonhold and Leasehold Reform Act (2002 c.15), s. 180, Sch. 14. Date in force (in relation to England only): September 30, 2003, see SI 2003/1986. Date in force (in relation to Wales): March 30, 2004, see SI 2004/669.
Replace Footnote 460 with the following: Repealed by Commonhold and Leasehold Reform Act (2002 c.15), Sch. 13, para. 13(3). Date in force (in relation to England only): September 30, 2003, see SI 2003/1986. Date in force (in relation to Wales): March 30, 2004, see SI 2004/669.

Jurisdictions of leasehold valuation tribunals in relation to enfranchisement, etc. of Crown land

898–899   Replace section 88(2)(c) and (3)–(5), (7) with the following:

(c) it is agreed between—
(i) the appropriate authority and the tenant, and
(ii) all other persons (if any) whose interests would fall to be represented in proceedings brought under that Part for the determination of that question by such a tribunal,
that question should be determined by such a tribunal, a [leasehold valuation tribunal][462] shall have jurisdiction to determine that question.

(3) [...][463]

(4) [. . .]463A
(5) [. . .]463B
(7) [. . .]464

Replace Footnote 462 with the following: Words substituted by Commonhold and Leasehold Reform Act (2002 c.15), s. 176, Sch. 13, para. 14. Date in force (in relation to England): September 30, 2003, see SI 2003/1986. Date in force (in relation to Wales): March 30, 2004, see SI 2004/669.
Replace Footnote 463 with the following: Repealed by Commonhold and Leasehold Reform Act (2002 c.15), s. 180, Sch. 14. Date in force (in relation to England): September 30, 2003, see SI 2003/1986. Date in force (in relation to Wales): March 30, 2004, see SI 2004/669.
Add new Footnote 463A: Repealed by Commonhold and Leasehold Reform Act (2002 c.15), s. 180, Sch. 14. Date in force (in relation to England only): September 30, 2003, see SI 2003/1986. Date in force (in relation to Wales): March 30, 2004, see SI 2004/669.
Add new Footnote 463B: Repealed by Commonhold and Leasehold Reform Act (2002 c.15), s. 180, Sch. 14. Date in force (in relation to England only): September 30, 2003, see SI 2003/1986. Date in force (in relation to Wales): March 30, 2004, see SI 2004/669.
Replace Footnote 464 with the following: Repealed by Commonhold and Leasehold Reform Act (2002 c.15), s. 180, Sch. 14. Date in force (in relation to England only): September 30, 2003, see SI 2003/1986. Date in force (in relation to Wales): March 30, 2004, see SI 2004/669.

Jurisdiction of leasehold valuation tribunals
Replace section 91 with the following: 899–902

91.—(1) [. . .]465 Any question arising in relation to any of the matters specified in subsection (2) shall, in default of agreement, be determined by [a leasehold valuation tribunal]466

(2) Those matters are—

    (a)   the terms of acquisition relating to—
        (i) any interest which is to be acquired by a nominee purchaser in pursuance of Chapter I, or
        (ii) any new lease which is to be granted to a tenant in pursuance of Chapter II,
        including in particular any matter which needs to be determined for the purposes of any provision of Schedule 6 or 13;
    (b)   the terms of any lease which is to be granted in accordance with section 36 and Schedule 9;
    (c)   the amount of any payment falling to be made by virtue of section 18(2);
    [(ca) the amount of any compensation payable under section 37A;]467
    [(cb) the amount of any compensation payable under section 61A;].468
    (d)   the amount of any costs payable by any person or persons by virtue of any provision of Chapter I or II and, in the case of costs to which section 33(1) or 60(1) applies, the liability of any person or persons by virtue of any such provision to pay any such costs; and
    (e)   the apportionment between two or more persons of any amount (whether of costs or otherwise) payable by virtue of any such provision.

(3) [. . .]468A
(4) [. . .]468B
(5) [. . .]468C

(6) [. . .]^468D

(7) [. . .]^468E

(8) [. . .]^469

(9) A leasehold valuation tribunal may, when determining the property in which any interest is to be acquired in pursuance of a notice under section 13 or 42, specify in its determination property which is less extensive than that specified in that notice.

(10) [. . .]^470

(11) In this section—

> "the nominee purchaser" and "the participating tenants" have the same meaning as in Chapter I;
> "the terms of acquisition" shall be construed in accordance with section 24(8) or section 48(7), as appropriate;

[. . .]^471

Replace Footnote 465 with the following: Words Repealed by Commonhold and Leasehold Reform Act (2002 c.15), s. 180, Sch. 14. Date in force (in relation to England only): September 30, 2003, see SI 2003/1986. Date in force (in relation to Wales): March 30, 2004, see SI 2004/669.

Replace Footnote 466 with the following: Words substituted by Commonhold and Leasehold Reform Act (2002 c.15), s. 176, Sch. 13, para. 15. Date in force (in relation to England only): September 30, 2003, see SI 2003/1986. Date in force (in relation to Wales): March 30, 2004, see SI 2004/669.

Replace Footnote 467 with the following: Added by Housing Act (1996 c.52), Sch. 11 para. 2(2).

Replace Footnote 468 with the following: Added by Housing Act (1996 c.52), Sch. 11 para. 3(2).

Add new Footnote 468A: Repealed by Commonhold and Leasehold Reform Act (2002 c.15), s. 180, Sch. 14. Date in force (in relation to England only): September 30, 2003, see SI 2003/1986. Date in force (in relation to Wales): March 30, 2004, see SI 2004/669.

Add new Footnote 468B: Repealed by Commonhold and Leasehold Reform Act (2002 c.15), s. 180, Sch. 14. Date in force (in relation to England only): September 30, 2003, see SI 2003/1986. Date in force (in relation to Wales): March 30, 2004, see SI 2004/669.

Add new Footnote 468C: Repealed by Commonhold and Leasehold Reform Act (2002 c.15), s. 180, Sch. 14. Date in force (in relation to England only): September 30, 2003, see SI 2003/1986. Date in force (in relation to Wales): March 30, 2004, see SI 2004/669.

Add new Footnote 468D: Repealed by Commonhold and Leasehold Reform Act (2002 c.15), s. 180, Sch. 14. Date in force (in relation to England only): September 30, 2003, see SI 2003/1986. Date in force (in relation to Wales): March 30, 2004, see SI 2004/669.

Add new Footnote 468E: Repealed by Commonhold and Leasehold Reform Act (2002 c.15), s. 180, Sch. 14. Date in force (in relation to England only): September 30, 2003, see SI 2003/1986. Date in force (in relation to Wales): March 30, 2004, see SI 2004/669.

Replace Footnote 469 with the following: Repealed by Commonhold and Leasehold Reform Act (2002 c.15), s. 180, Sch. 14. Date in force (in relation to England only): September 30, 2003, see SI 2003/1986. Date in force (in relation to Wales): March 30, 2004, see SI 2004/669.

Replace Footnote 470 with the following: Repealed by Commonhold and Leasehold Reform Act (2002 c.15), s. 180, Sch. 14. Date in force (in relation to England only): September 30, 2003, see SI 2003/1986. Date in force (in relation to Wales): March 30, 2004, see SI 2004/669.

Replace Footnote 471 with the following: Repealed by Commonhold and Leasehold Reform Act (2002 c.15), s. 180, Sch. 14. Date in force (in relation to England only): September 30, 2003, see SI 2003/1986. Date in force (in relation to Wales): March 30, 2004, see SI 2004/669.

Registration of notices, applications and orders under Chapters I and II

908 Replace section 97 with the following:

97.—(1) No lease shall be registrable under the Land Charges Act 1972 or be taken to be an estate contract within the meaning of that Act by reason of any rights or obligations of the tenant or landlord which may arise under Chapter I or

II, and any right of a tenant arising from a notice given under section 13 or 42 shall not be [capable of falling within paragraph 2 of Schedule 1 or 3 to the Land Registration Act 2002];[482A] but a notice given under section 13 or 42 shall be registrable under the Land Charges Act 1972, or may be the subject of a notice [under the Land Registration Act 2002],[482B] as if it were an estate contract.

(2) The Land Charges Act 1972 and the [Land Registration Act 2002][482C]

(a) shall apply in relation to an order made under section 26(1) or 50(1) as they apply in relation to an order affecting land which is made by the court for the purpose of enforcing a judgment or recognisance; and

(b) shall apply in relation to an application for such an order as they apply in relation to other pending land actions.

(3) [. . .][482D]

Add new Footnote 482A: Words substituted by Land Registration Act (2002 c.9), Sch. 11, para. 30.

Add new Footnote 482B: Words substituted by Land Registration Act (2002 c.9), Sch. 11, para. 30.

Add new Footnote 482C: Words substituted by Land Registration Act (2002 c.9), Sch. 11, para. 30.

Add new Footnote 482D: Repealed by Land Registration Act (2002 c.9), Sch. 13.

Notices

Replace section 99(5) with the following: **910**

(5) Any notice which is given under Chapter I or II by any tenants or tenant must—

(a) if it is a notice given under section 13 or 42, be signed by each of the tenants, or (as the case may be) by the tenant, by whom it is given; and

(b) in any other case, be signed by or on behalf of each of the tenants, or (as the case may be) by or on behalf of the tenant, by whom it is given.

General interpretation of Part I

Add to Footnote 483: Definition of "rent assessment committee" repealed in Wales on March 30, 2004, see SI 2004/669.   **911**

Section 32   Schedule 6

Interpretation and operation of Schedule

The definition of "the valuation date" in Paragraph 1(1) was repealed by the Commonhold and Leasehold Reform Act 2002, s. 180 and Sch. 14 with effect from 28 February 2005 in England and 31 May 2005 in Wales. By s. 126(1) of the 2002 Act, the references to "the valuation date" should be substituted by "the relevant date". These references occur in paragraphs 3(1), 3(2), 3(4), 4(3)(b), 7(7), 7(8) and 7(9).   **930–935**

Freeholder's share of marriage value

Add a footnote to paragraph 4(2): During the period beginning with 28 February 2005 (in England) and 31 May 2005 (in Wales) and ending with the date on which ss. 121–124   **932** come fully into force, paragraph 4(2) shall have effect as if, for "participating tenants", there were substituted "persons who are participating tenants immediately before a binding contract is entered into in pursuance of the initial notice." SI 2004 No. 3056, art. 4(1), SI 2005 No. 1353, art 3(1).

Apportionment of marriage value

940   Footnote 528: replace text with the following: Words substituted by Housing Act (1996 c.52), Sch. 10, para. 18(4).

Section 27   Schedule 10

Provisions relating to secure tenants following leaseback

954   Replace last word on this page for "tenancy".

APPENDIX 1H

Commonhold and Leasehold Reform Act 2002

122.—RTE Companies
In section 4B(1)(b) substitute "RTM" for "RAM".   **974**

Insert section 159 after section 149:   **985**

159.—Charges under estate management schemes
(1) This section applies where a scheme under—

(a) section 19 of the 1967 Act (estate management schemes in connection with enfranchisement under that Act),
(b) Chapter 4 of Part 1 of the 1993 Act (estate management schemes in connection with enfranchisement under the 1967 Act or Chapter 1 of Part 1 of the 1993 Act), or
(c) section 94(6) of the 1993 Act (corresponding schemes in relation to areas occupied under leases from Crown),

includes provision imposing on persons occupying or interested in property an obligation to make payments ("estate charges").

(2) A variable estate charge is payable only to the extent that the amount of the charge is reasonable; and "variable estate charge" means an estate charge which is neither—

(a) specified in the scheme, nor
(b) calculated in accordance with a formula specified in the scheme.

(3) Any person on whom an obligation to pay an estate charge is imposed by the scheme may apply to a leasehold valuation tribunal for an order varying the scheme in such manner as is specified in the application on the grounds that—

(a) any estate charge specified in the scheme is unreasonable, or
(b) any formula specified in the scheme in accordance with which any estate charge is calculated is unreasonable.

(4) If the grounds on which the application was made are established to the satisfaction of the tribunal, it may make an order varying the scheme in such manner as is specified in the order.
(5) The variation specified in the order may be—

(a) the variation specified in the application, or
(b) such other variation as the tribunal thinks fit.

(6) An application may be made to a leasehold valuation tribunal for a determination whether an estate charge is payable by a person and, if it is, as to—

(a) the person by whom it is payable,
(b) the person to whom it is payable,
(c) the amount which is payable,
(d) the date at or by which it is payable, and
(e) the manner in which it is payable.

(7) Subsection (6) applies whether or not any payment has been made.

(8) The jurisdiction conferred on a leasehold valuation tribunal in respect of any matter by virtue of subsection (6) is in addition to any jurisdiction of a court in respect of the matter.

(9) No application under subsection (6) may be made in respect of a matter which—

(a) has been agreed or admitted by the person concerned,
(b) has been, or is to be, referred to arbitration pursuant to a post-dispute arbitration agreement to which that person is a party,
(c) has been the subject of determination by a court, or
(d) has been the subject of determination by an arbitral tribunal pursuant to a post-dispute arbitration agreement.

(10) But the person is not to be taken to have agreed or admitted any matter by reason only of having made any payment.

(11) An agreement (other than a post-dispute arbitration agreement) is void in so far as it purports to provide for a determination—

(a) in a particular manner, or
(b) on particular evidence, of any question which may be the subject matter of an application under subsection (6).

(12) In this section—

"post-dispute arbitration agreement", in relation to any matter, means an arbitration agreement made after a dispute about the matter has arisen, and
"arbitration agreement" and "arbitral tribunal" have the same meanings as in Part 1 of the Arbitration Act 1996 (c.23).

SCHEDULES

Schedule 8   Section 124

995 Replace paragraph 37(12) with the following:
(12) For paragraph 16 (and the heading before it) substitute—

"Effect on initial notice of member's lack of qualification

16. Where any of the members of the RTE company by which an initial notice is given was not the qualifying tenant of a flat contained in the premises at the relevant date even though his name was stated in the notice, the notice is not invalidated on that account, so long as a sufficient number of qualifying tenants of flats contained in the premises were members of the company at that date; and for this purpose a "sufficient number" is a number (greater than one) which is not less than one-half of the total number of flats contained in the premises at that date."

APPENDIX 1I

Law of Property Act 1925

Enlargement of residue of long terms into fee simple estates

1004 Replace section 153(4) with the following:

(4) A rent not exceeding the yearly sum of one pound which has not been collected or paid for a continuous period of twenty years or upwards shall, for the purposes of this section, be deemed to have ceased to be payable [. . .][585A] [. . .][585B]

Add new Footnote 585A: Substituted by Statute Law Repeals Act (2004 c.14), Sch. 1, para. 12.
Add new Footnote 585B: Repealed by Statute Law Repeals Act (2004 c.14), Sch. 1, para. 12.

APPENDIX 1J

Civil Partnership Act 2004

Housing and tenancies

Schedule 8 amends certain enactments relating to housing and tenancies.   **1006**

Section 81   Schedule 8

HOUSING AND TENANCIES

Leasehold Reform Act 1967 (c.88)

3. In section 1(1ZC)(c) (which refers to section 149(6) of the Law of Property Act 1925), after "terminable after a death or marriage" insert "or the formation of a civil partnership".

4. In section 1B (which refers to a tenancy granted so as to become terminable by notice after a death or marriage), for "a death or marriage" substitute "a death, a marriage or the formation of a civil partnership".

5.—(1) Amend section 3(1) (meaning of "long tenancy") as follows.

(2) In the words describing section 149(6) of the Law of Property Act 1925, after "terminable after a death or marriage" insert "or the formation of a civil partnership".

(3) In the proviso (exclusion of certain tenancies terminable by notice after death or marriage)—

    (a) for "a death or marriage" substitute "a death, a marriage or the formation of a civil partnership", and

    (b) in paragraph (a), after "marriage of" insert ", or the formation of a civil partnership by,".

6.—(1) Amend section 7 (rights of members of family succeeding to tenancy on death) as follows.

(2) In subsection (7) ("family member"), for "wife or husband" (in each place) substitute "spouse or civil partner".

(3) In subsection (8) (surviving spouse's rights on intestacy)—

    (a) in paragraph (a), for "wife or husband" substitute "spouse or civil partner", and

    (b) in paragraph (b), for "husband or wife" substitute "spouse or civil partner".

7. In section 18(3) (members of landlord's family whose residential rights exclude enfranchisement or extension), for "wife or husband" (in each place) substitute "spouse or civil partner".

Leasehold Reform, Housing and Urban Development Act 1993 (c.28)

47.—(1) Amend section 7 (meaning of "long lease") as follows.

(2) In subsection (1)(b) (which refers to section 149(6) of the Law of Property Act 1925), after "terminable after a death or marriage" insert "or the formation of a civil partnership".

(3) In subsection (2) (exclusion of certain leases terminable by notice after death or marriage)—

    (a) for "a death or marriage" substitute "a death, a marriage or the formation of a civil partnership", and

    (b) in paragraph (a), after "marriage of" insert ", or the formation of a civil partnership by,".

48. In section 10(5) (members of family of resident landlord), for "wife or husband" (in each place) substitute "spouse or civil partner".

These provisions came into force on December 5, 2005.

STATUTORY INSTRUMENTS

APPENDIX 2A

Leasehold Reform (Enfranchisement and Extension) Regulations 1967

(SI 1967/1879)

Please note: In Regulation 1(2) the word "context" should not be broken.   **1007**

Add to Footnote 1: Words inserted (in relation to Wales) by SI 2004/699, reg. 3.   **1008**
Add to Footnote 2: Added (in relation to Wales) by SI 2004/699, reg. 3.

Add to Footnote 3: Words inserted (in relation to Wales) by SI 2004/699, reg. 3.   **1012**
Add to Footnote 4: Added (in relation to Wales) by SI 2004/699, reg. 3.

APPENDIX 2C

Leasehold Reform (Collective Enfranchisement and Lease Renewal) Regulations 1993

(SI 1993/2407)

SCHEDULE 1

COLLECTIVE ENFRANCHISEMENT

Delete paragraph 2(2)

SCHEDULE 2

Add after para 4(1);

> *[(1) The landlord may require the tenant to deduce his title to his tenancy, by giving him notice within the period of twenty one days beginning with the relevant date.]*[5AA]

Add to Footnote 5: Paragraph (2) deleted by SI 2004/670, reg. 3 in relation to Wales with effect from March 31, 2004.
Add new Footnote 5AA: Substituted by SI 2004/670 in relation to Wales only.

APPENDIX 2E

Lands Tribunal Rules 1996

(SI 1996/1022)

Interpretation

In rule 2(1) amend definition of "registrar":   **1028**

> "the registrar" means the registrar of the Lands Tribunal or, as respects any
> powers or functions of the registrar, an office of the Lands Tribunal
> authorised by the Lord Chancellor, [after consulting the Lord Chief
> Justice,][6A] to exercise those powers or functions;

Insert after rule 2(1)

[(1A) The Lord Chief Justice may nominate a judicial office holder (as defined
in section 109(4) of the Constitutional Reform Act 2005) to exercise his functions referred to in the definition of "the registrar" in paragraph (1).][6B]

Add new Footnote 6A: Words substituted by SI 2006/680.
Add new Footnote 6B: Added by SI 2006/680.

Insert rule 5A as amended as follows:

[Application of Part IIA

[**5A** Part IIA applies to an application to the Lands Tribunal for permission to   **1029**
appeal—

(a) under section 175 of the Commonhold and Leasehold Reform Act 2002,
against a decision of the Leasehold Valuation Tribunal; or
(b) under section 231 of the Housing Act 2004, against a decision of the
residential property tribunal.][6C]

Add new Footnote 6C: Rule 5A substituted by SI 2066/880.

Replace rules 5B–6 with the following:

PART IIA

[APPLICATIONS FOR PERMISSION TO APPEAL

[Interpretation

[**5B.**—(A) In this Part "first-tier tribunal" means—   **1029–**
                                                                                    1032

(a) in relation to an appeal under section 175 of the Commonhold and
Leasehold Reforms Act 2002, the Leasehold Valuation Tribunal; and

(b) in relation to an appeal under section 231 of the Housing Act 2004, the
residential property tribunal.][6D]

(1) A respondent to an application for [permission][6E] to appeal is any party in
the proceedings before [the first-tier tribunal],[6F] other than the applicant, who
was present or represented at the hearing [before the first-tier tribunal] or, where
the proceedings were determined without a hearing, [made representations in
writing to that tribunal].
(2) A respondent to an application for [permission][6E] to appeal shall not be a
respondent to any subsequent appeal unless he gives notice of intention to
respond to the appeal in accordance with rule 7.][7]

[Application for permission to appeal
   5C.—(1) A person ('the applicant') may only apply to the Lands Tribunal for
[permission][7A] to appeal if he has made an application to the [first-tier tribunal][7B]
for such [permission][7A] and that application has been refused.
   (2) An application for [permission][7A] must be made to the Lands Tribunal
within [14][7C] days of the date on which the decision of the [first-tier tribunal][7B]
to refuse [permission][7A] to appeal was sent to the applicant.
   (3) The application for [permission][7A] shall contain—

   (a) the name and address of the applicant;
   (b) the name and address of every respondent
   (c) the grounds of appeal against the decision in respect of which [permis-
        sion][7A] is sought;
   (d) where the applicant is represented, the name, address and profession of
        the representative; and
   (e) the signature of the applicant or his representative and the date the
        application was signed.

   (4) The application for [permission][7A] shall be accompanied by—

   (a) a copy of the decision against which [permission][7A] is being sought.
   (b) a copy of the decision of the [first-tier tribunal][7B] refusing leave to
        appeal;
   (c) the fee payable to the Lands Tribunal in respect of the proposed
        appeal.

   (5) The applicant shall deliver or send the application for [permission][7A] to
appeal to the Lands Tribunal together with sufficient copies for service upon each
respondent.
   (6) Upon receiving an application for [permission][7A] to appeal the registrar
shall—

   (a) serve a copy of the application on each respondent;
   (b) inform the applicant of the date on which this was done; and
   (c) enter the details of the application in the register of appeals.

(7) The registrar shall, when serving a copy of the application, notify each respondent of the time limit, specified by the Tribunal, within which any written representations relating to the application must be made to the Tribunal.]⁸

[Determination of application

5D.—(1) The Tribunal shall determine an application for [permission]⁸ᴬ without a hearing unless it considers that there are special circumstances which make a hearing necessary or desirable.

(2) The registrar shall serve on the applicant and each respondent a notice regarding the decision of the Tribunal on the application for [permission]⁸ᴬ].⁹

[Refusal of permission to appeal

5E.—If the Tribunal refuses [permission]⁹ᴬ to appeal the registrar shall refund to the applicant the fee paid in respect of the appeal.]¹⁰

[Permission to appeal

5F.—(1) If the Tribunal grants [permission]¹⁰ᴬ to appeal it may do so on such conditions as it thinks fit including the conditions relating to the costs of the appeal.

(2) The registrar shall note in the register of appeals that the appeal is proceeding unless the applicant notifies him, within 14 days of the date of service of the notice recording the decision to grant [permission]¹⁰ᴬ, that he does not wish to proceed with the appeal.

(3) The registrar shall serve notice on each respondent that the appeal is proceeding with details of the number of the appeal entered on the register which shall constitute the title of the appeal.]¹¹

[Application of Part III (Appeals)

5G.—Where an appeal proceeds following the grant of [permission]¹¹ᴬ to appeal under this Part—

(a) rule 6 shall not apply to the appeal; and
(b) rule 7 shall apply as if the reference to the notice of appeal was a reference to the notice that the appeal is proceeding referred to in rule 5F(3).]¹²

[Application of Part VII (General Procedure)

5H.—In Part VIII, reference to an appeal shall include reference to an application for [permission]¹²ᴬ to appeal under this Part.]¹³]¹⁴

Add new Footnote 6D: Added by SI 2006/680 in force since April 28, 2006.
Add new Footnote 6E: Word substituted by SI 2003/2945, r.6 (in force in relation to England only from December 7, 2003).
Add new Footnote 6F: Words substituted for "Leasehold Valuation Tribunal" by SI 2003/2945.
Replace Footnote 7 with the following: Added by SI 1997/1965, r.4.
Add new Footnote 7A: Word substituted by SI 2003/2945, r.6.
Add new Footnote 7B: Words substituted by SI 2006/880.
Add new Footnote 7C: Substituted for 28 by SI 2006/880, r.4(2) in force since April 28, 2006.
Replace Footnote 8 with the following: Added by SI 1997/1965, r.4.
Add new Footnote 8A: Word substituted by SI 2003/2945, r.6.

128   APPENDIX 2E

Replace Footnote 9 with the following: Added by SI 1997/1965, r.4.
Add new Footnote 9A: Word substituted by SI 2003/2945, r.6.
Replace Footnote 10 with the following: Added by SI 1997/1965, r.4.
Add new Footnote 10A: Word substituted by SI 2003/2945, r.6.
Replace Footnote 11 with the following: Added by SI 1997/1965, r.4.
Add new Footnote 11A: Word substituted by SI 2003/2945, r.6.
Replace Footnote 12 with the following: Added by SI 1997/1965, r.4.
Add new Footnote 12A: Word substituted by SI 2003/2945, r.6.
Replace Footnote 13 with the following: Added by SI 1997/1965, r.4.
Replace Footnote 14 with the following: Added by SI 1997/1965, r.4.

PART III

APPEALS

Notice of appeal

6.—[(1) An appeal to the Lands Tribunal shall be made by sending to the registrar a written notice indicating an intention to appeal so that it is received by the registrar—

(a) within 28 days of the date on which the decision appealed against ('the disputed decision') was sent to the applicant, or within such other time as is prescribed by the enactment conferring the right to appeal; or

(b) [subject to paragraph (1B)]^{14A} where the appeal is made following the grant of [permission]^{14B} to appeal [. . .],^{14C} within 28 days of the date on which the decision granting [permission]^{14D} to appeal was sent to the applicant.]^{15}

Insert new (1A), (1B):

[(1A) Paragraph (1B) applies to—

(a) an appeal under section 175 of the Commonhold and Leasehold Reform Act 2002 against a decision of the Leasehold Reform Act 2002 against a decision of the Leasehold Valuation Tribunal; or

(b) an appeal under section 231 of the Housing Act 2004 against a decision of the residential property tribunal.

[(1B) Subject to rule 35A, if it is satisfied that it is in the interests of the justice to do so, the Tribunal may direct—

(a) that a shorter period be substituted for the period of 28 days in paragraph (1)(b); or

(b) that the application to the first-tier tribunal for permission to appeal shall stand as notice under paragraph (1).]^{15A}

Insert after (1B):

[(2) Where the notice referred to in paragraph (1) does not conform with the requirements set out in paragraph (3), the appellant shall, within such time as the registrar may direct, send to the registrar a notice which does so conform.

(3) The notice of appeal shall state that it is a notice of appeal and shall contain—

    (a) the name and address of the appellant;

    (b) the date and any reference number of the disputed decision and the name and address of the Authority;

    (c) the grounds of appeal;

    (d) where the appellant is represented, the name, address and profession of the representative; and

    (e) the signature of the appellant or his representative and the date the notice was signed.

[(4) The appellant shall attach to the notice of appeal—

    (a) a copy of the disputed decision; and

    (b) where the appeal is made following grant of [permission][15A] to appeal by the authority, a copy of the decision granting [permission][15B] to appeal; and

    (c) where the appeal relates to a rating appeal, a copy of the proposal or determination that was the subject of the proceedings which led to the disputed decision.][16]

(5) The appellant shall deliver or send the notice of appeal to the Lands Tribunal together with sufficient copies for service upon each of the parties to the proceedings which led to the disputed decision and upon the authority, and where appropriate, the valuation officer.

(6) Upon receiving a notice of appeal the registrar shall—

    (a) enter particulars of the appeal in the [register of appeals];[17]

    (b) serve a copy of the notice on the parties to the proceedings which led to the disputed decision other than the appellant, on the authority and, where applicable, on the valuation officer and inform the appellant of the date on which this was done; and

    (c) inform the appellant and all persons on whom a copy of the notice of appeal is served of the number of the appeal entered on the Register which shall constitute the title of the appeal.][17A]

Substitute for r 7(2):

(2) [Subject to paragraph (2B), the notice of intention to respond][17B] shall be **1033** served on the registrar and the appellant within 28 days of the date of service of the copy of the notice of appeal.

Insert after r 7(2):

[(2A) Paragraph (2B) applies to—

    (a) an appeal under section 175 of the Commonhold and Leasehold Reform Act 2002 against a decision of the Leasehold Valuation Tribunal; or

130   APPENDIX 2E

(b) an appeal under section 231 of the Housing Act 2004 against a decision
     of the residential property tribunal.][17C]

(2B) Subject to rule 35A, if it is satisfied that it is in the interests of justice to
do so, the Tribunal may direct that a shorter period be substituted for the period
of 28 days in paragraph (2).][17D]

Substitute for r 8(2):
  [(2) Subject to paragraph (4B), within 28 days of service][17E] of a notice of
intention to respond, the appellant shall serve on the respondent from whom it is
received, a statement of his case, including full particulars of the facts relied upon
and any points of law on which he intends to rely at the hearing.

Substitute for r 8(3)
  [(3) Subject to paragraph(4B), within 28 days of service][17F] of the appellant's
statement, a respondent shall serve on the appellant a reply stating his case
including full paticulars of the facts relied upon and any points of law on which
he intends to rely at the hearing.

Substitute for r 8(4):
  [Subject to paragraph (4B), where a party receives][17G] from the registrar a
copy of a notice of intention to respond from another party in accordance with
rule 7(3), he shall, within 28 days of service of such notice on him, send to that
other party a copy of the reply referred to in paragraph (3).

Insert new (4A) and (4B) after r 8(4):
  [(4A) Paragraph (4B) applies to—

(a) an appeal under section 175 of the Commonhold and Leasehold Reform
     Act 2002 against a decision of the Leasehold Valuation Tribunal; or
(b) an appeal under section 231 of the Housing Act 2004 against a decision
     of the residential property tribunal.][17H]

(4B) Subject to rule 35A, if it is satisfied that it is in the interests of justice to
do so, the Tribunal may direct that a shorter period be substituted for the period
of 28 days in paragraph (2), (3) or (4).][17I]

Add new Footnote 14A: Words added by SI 2006/880.
Add new Footnote 14B: Word substituted by SI 2003/2945, r.6 (in force in relation to England only
from December 7, 2003).
Add new Footnote 14C: Omitted by SI 2006/886 from April 28, 2006.
Add new Footnote 14D: Words substituted by SI 2003/2945, r.6.
Replace Footnote 15 with the following: Rule 6(1) substituted by SI 1997/1965, r.5.
Add new Footnote 15A: Added by SI 2006/880, r.6.
Add new Footnote 15B: Aded by SI 2006/880, r.5(2).
Replace Footnote 16 with the following: Substituted by SI 1997/1965, r.6.
Replace Footnote 17 with the following: Words substituted by SI 1997/1965, r.7.
Add Footnote 17A; Words added by SI 2006/880, r.6(1), in force since April 28, 2006.
Add Footnote 17B: Added by SI 2006/880, r.6(2), in force since April 28, 2006.
Add Footnote 17C: Added by SI 2006/880, r.7(1).
Add Footnote 17D: Added by SI 2006/880, r.7(1).
Add Footnote 17E: Added by SI 2006/880, r.7(3) in force since April 28, 2006.

PART VII

REFERENCES BY CONSENT

Insert rule 26A following (26)(g) as follows:

[**26A.**—The person referring the matter to the Lands Tribunal shall, at the time **1034**
the reference is made, supply the Lands Tribunal with copies of the arbitration
agreement and any other written agreement relevant to the manner of arbitration.]¹⁹

Replace Footnote 19 with the following: Added by SI 1997/1965, r.8.

PART VIII

GENERAL PROCEDURE

Simplified procedure
Replace rule 28(11) with the following: **1036**

(11) No award shall be made in relation to the costs of the proceedings except
in cases to which section 4 of the 1961 Act [or subsections (6) and (7) of section
175 of the Commonhold and Leasehold Reform Act 2002 apply]¹⁹ᴬ, save that the
Tribunal may make an award of costs.

Add new Footnote 19A: Words substituted for former word "apply" by SI 2003/2945, r.7 (in force
in relation to England only from December 7, 2003 and in Wales from March 30, 2004).

Shortening of time, etc.
Insert rule 35A following (34)(3) as follows: **1039**

[**35A.** —(1) In this rule "urgency direction" means a direction under rule
6(1B), 7(2B) or 8(4B).

(2) The Tribunal may make an urgency direction—

(a) on application of a party, or
(b) on its own initiative.

(3) Paragraphs (4) to (8) apply, and rule 38 does not apply, where a party
applies for an urgency direction

(4) The application shall be made in writing an shall state the title of the
proceedings, and the grounds upon which the application is made.

(5) If the application is made with the consent of all parties, it shall be
accompanied by consents signed by or on behalf of the parties.

(6) If the application is not made with the consent of every party the applicant
shall serve a copy of the proposed application on every other party before it is
made and the application shall state that this has been done.

(7) Subject to paragraph (8), the Tribunal shall give notice in writing to the parties other than the applicant inviting them to make representations in writing in relation to the application.

(8) Paragraph (7) does not apply where the Tribunal, having considered the application and the grounds upon which it is made, decides to refuse the application.

(9) Where the Tribunal proposes to make an urgency direction on its own initiative it shall give notice in writing to the parties—

  (a) of the direction which it proposes to make; and

  (b) inviting the parties to make representations in writing in relation to the proposal.

(10) The notice given under paragraph (7) or (9) may specify a date by which representations are to be made.

(11) Before making an urgency direction the Tribunal shall consider all the representations that it has received.][22A]

Add new Footnote 22A: Added by SI 2006/880, r.8.

Costs

1045   Replace rule 52(1) with the following:

Subject to the provisions of section 4 of the 1961 Act [subsections (6) and (7) of section 175 of the Commonhold and Leasehold Reform Act 2002][26A] and of rule 28(11), the costs of and incidental to any proceedings shall be in the discretion of the Tribunal.

Add new Footnote 26A: Words inserted by SI 2003/2945, r.8 (in force in England only from December 7, 2003 and in Wales from March 30, 2004).

APPENDIX 2I

Replace Appendix 2I with the following: **1133–**
                                                                           1147

Lands Tribunal Practice Directions, 11 May 2006

1. Introduction

1.1 Procedure in the Tribunal is governed by the Lands Tribunal Rules 1996 (SI 1996 No 1022), as amended by the Lands Tribunal (Amendment) Rules of 1997, 1998, 2003 and 2006 (SI 1997 No.1965, SI 1998 No.22, SI 2003 No.2945 and SI 2006 No.880). Practice Directions, issued from time to time by the President, contain information on the way in which the procedure contained in the rules is operated. These Practice Directions supersede all those previously issued. They apply to all proceedings, including references by consent.

2. The overriding objective

2.1 The Civil Procedure Rules, which apply to the ordinary civil courts of law (the Court of Appeal, the High Court and the county courts), have no application in the Tribunal. Nevertheless in following its procedures the Tribunal does so on the basis of the same overriding objective as that in the CPR. The overriding objective is to follow procedures that enable the Tribunal to deal with cases justly. Dealing with a case justly includes, so far as is practicable—

    (a) ensuring that the parties are on an equal footing;

    (b) saving expense;

    (c) dealing with the case in ways which are proportionate—

        (i) to the amount of money involved;

        (ii) to the importance of the case;

        (iii) to the complexity of the issues; and

        (iv) to the financial position of each party;

    (d) ensuring that it is dealt with expeditiously and fairly; and

    (e) allotting to it an appropriate share of the Tribunal's resources, while taking into account the need to allot resources to other cases.

2.2 The Tribunal expects parties to assist it to further the overriding objective.

3. Case management
3.1 Introduction

Every case will be assigned to one of four procedures, as soon as the Tribunal or the Registrar has sufficient information to enable this to be done:

    (a) the standard procedure;

    (b) the special procedure;

(c) the simplified procedure;

(d) the written representations procedure. Any views expressed by the parties on the procedure to which a case should be assigned will be taken into account.

3.2 Special procedure

A case will be assigned to the **special procedure** if it requires case management by a Member in view of its complexity, the amount in issue or its wider importance. Once a case has been allocated to a Member (or Members) under the special procedure, the Member(s) will order a pre-trial review to be held under LT rule 39. The purpose of the pre-trial review is to ensure so far as practicable that all appropriate directions are given for the fair, expeditious and economical conduct of the proceedings. Where appropriate a date for the hearing will be fixed at the pre-trial review and the steps which the parties are required to take, and further pre-trial reviews, will be timetabled by reference to this date. Before the pre-trial reviews the parties will be asked to the extent that they are able to do so at that stage, to identify the issues in the case, and to state the areas of expertise of each expert witness that they propose to rely on and the general scope of his evidence. Each party should consider whether it is appropriate to make application under LT rule 43 (determination of a preliminary issue) and LT rule 42 (leave to call more than the permitted number of expert witnesses) and it should identify, and where necessary make application for, any other order that it wishes the Tribunal to make at the pre-trial review.

3.3 Simplified procedure

LT rule 28 provides for the assignment of a case to the **simplified procedure**. The purpose of this procedure is to provide for the speedy and economical determination of cases in which no substantial issue of law or valuation practice, or substantial conflict of fact, is likely to arise. It is often suitable where the amount at stake is small. The procedure is initiated by a direction of a Member or the Registrar, made with the consent of the claimant, appellant or applicant, that the proceedings should be determined under this rule. There is provision for any other party to object and for determining such objection as an interlocutory matter under LT rule 38.

3.4 The objective is to move to a hearing as quickly as possible and with the minimum of formality and cost. In most cases a date for the hearing, normally about 3 months ahead, will be fixed immediately, and the parties will be required to file a statement of case and a reply. They must, not later than 28 days before the hearing, exchange copies of all documents on which they intend to rely, and experts' reports must be exchanged not later than 14 days before the hearing. The hearing is informal and strict rules of evidence do not apply. It will almost always be completed in a single day. Except in compensation cases, to which particular statutory provisions on costs apply, an award of costs is made only in exceptional circumstances.

3.5 Written representation procedure

Under LT rule 27 the Tribunal may, with the consent of the parties to the proceedings, order that the proceedings be determined without an oral hearing. Such an order for the **written representation procedure** to be followed will only be made if the Tribunal, having regard to the issues in the case and the desirability of minimising costs, is of the view that oral evidence and argument can properly be dispensed with. Directions will be given to the parties relating to the lodging of representations and documents, and the Member allocated to the case will if necessary carry out a site inspection before giving his written decision.

3.6 Standard procedure

The **standard procedure** applies in all other cases. Under this procedure case management will be in the hands of the Registrar. He will look to hold a pre-trial review at the earliest time that it appears appropriate to do so, and he will give directions tailored to the requirements of the particular case. These directions may, as appropriate, use elements of the special procedure (for example, time-tabling through to the hearing date) or the simplified procedure.

3.7 At any time the Registrar, or the Member to whom the case has been allocated, may direct that it should be assigned to one of the other procedures, provided that any consent from a party that is required under LT rule 27 or rule 28 has been given.

3.8 At the time an appellant lodges his notice of appeal or a respondent his notice of intention to respond he will be asked to state to which of the procedures he suggests that the case should be assigned. The same course will be followed in relation to every party to a reference, and to the applicant and objectors in an application under Part V of the LT Rules.

4. Stay of proceedings pending negotiation or alternative dispute resolution (ADR)

4.1 At the time an appellant lodges his notice of appeal or a respondent his notice of intention to respond he will be asked to state whether he wishes the proceedings to be stayed to allow negotiations for a settlement to take place or an Alternative Dispute Resolution procedure to be followed. Parties to a reference also will be asked whether they wish the proceedings to be stayed for this purpose. Where both parties indicate such a wish, a stay of 4 weeks will normally be granted. If a longer period is asked for, the parties will need to satisfy the Tribunal that in the circumstances of the particular case this would be appropriate.

5. Appeals from Leasehold Valuation Tribunals

5.1 Introduction

In respect of applications to a leasehold valuation tribunal made after 30 September 2003 a party may appeal to the Lands Tribunal under section 175(1) of the Commonhold and Leasehold Reform Act 2002; but by section 175(2) it is provided that an appeal may only be made with the permission of the LVT or the Lands Tribunal.

5.2 Procedure in cases where permission required

Where permission is required it must first be sought from the LVT concerned: LT rule 5C(1). If the LVT grants permission, notice of appeal must be given to the Registrar of the Lands Tribunal within 28 days of the grant of permission to appeal: LT rule 6(1). There is power to extend the time limit (LT rule 35), but no extension will be granted unless there is justification for it. An urgency direction may be issued, upon application by a party or by the Lands Tribunal acting on its own initiative, to reduce this (and certain other) time limits: LT rule 35A; see further below.

5.3 Forms for the notice of appeal can be downloaded from the Lands Tribunal website or obtained from the Lands Tribunal. A completed form must be sent or delivered to the Lands Tribunal together with a copy of the disputed decision and a copy of the LVT's decision granting permission to appeal.

5.4 If the LVT refuses permission to appeal, application for permission may be made to the Lands Tribunal within 14 days of the decision of the LVT to refuse permission: LT rule 5C(2) (as amended). There is power to extend this time limit (LT rule 35), but no extension will be granted unless there is justification for it. Forms for the application can be obtained from the Lands Tribunal. These provide for the applicant to set out, in addition to their grounds of appeal, the reasons for the application for permission. It is for the applicant to satisfy the Lands Tribunal that permission to appeal should be given and their reasons should therefore be set out fully as provided for on the form. The application must be accompanied by a copy of the decision against which permission to appeal is being sought and a copy of the decision of the LVT refusing permission to appeal.

5.5 On receiving an application for permission to appeal, the Tribunal, unless it decides that permission should be refused without further representations, will serve a copy of the application on each respondent and will inform the applicant of the date when this was done. Respondents will be informed of the time limit specified by the Tribunal within which any written representations must be made. The Tribunal will consider any such representations and the applicant's reasons for his application and will decide whether to grant permission. Only in special circumstances will a hearing be held before a decision to grant or to refuse permission.

5.6 If the Tribunal grants permission, it may do so on such conditions as it thinks fit. In view of the limitation on the Tribunal's power to award costs contained in section 175(6) and (7) of the Commonhold and Leasehold Reform Act 2002, it will not be appropriate to impose conditions relating to costs. It would, however, be open to an appellant to undertake to pay all or part of a respondent's costs.

5.7 **Approach of the Tribunal to the grant of permission**
On the application form applicants are asked to specify whether their reasons for making the application fall within one or more of the following categories:

    (a) The decision shows that the LVT wrongly interpreted or wrongly applied the relevant law.

    (b) The decision shows that the LVT wrongly applied or misinterpreted or disregarded a relevant principle of valuation or other professional practice.

(c) The LVT took account of irrelevant considerations, or failed to take account of relevant consideration or evidence, or there was a substantial procedural defect.

(d) The point or points at issue is or are of potentially wide implication.

5.8 The application must make clear whether the appellant is seeking

(i) an appeal by way of review, or
(ii) an appeal by way of review, which if successful will involve a consequential re-hearing, or
(iii) an appeal by way of re-hearing.

Unless the application otherwise specifies, the application will be treated as an application for an appeal by way of review.

5.9 The Tribunal will grant permission to appeal only where it appears that there are reasonable grounds for concluding that the LVT may have been wrong for one or more of the reasons (a) to (c). In considering whether to grant permission on such grounds the importance of the point both to the decision itself and in terms of its wider implications will be a factor to be taken into consideration, in determining the proportionality and expedience of permitting an appeal to proceed. Where a successful appeal by review will necessitate a re-hearing, the Tribunal will have regard to the scope of such re-hearing in considering the proportionality of granting permission.

5.10 Procedure on appeal

The LT Rules Part III and Part VIII contain the procedure relating to appeals. Where an application for permission has been made and permission has been granted the application will be treated as the appellant's notice of appeal for the purposes of LT rule 6. Except in cases where the simplified procedure is followed under LT rule 28, the appellant will be required to serve a statement of case and each respondent will be required to serve a reply: see LT rule 8. Where a successful appeal by way of review will involve a consequential re-hearing of all or part of the evidence, unless the review is dealt with as a preliminary issue (see section 7 below), the review and the re-hearing will take place in the same hearing, and appropriate directions will be given for this purpose.

6. Appeals from Residential Property Tribunals
6.1 Introduction

Section 231(1) of the Housing Act 2004 provides that a party to the proceedings may appeal to the Lands Tribunal from a decision of a residential property tribunal (RPT); but section 23(2) stipulates that an appeal may only be made with the permission of the RPT or the Lands Tribunal.

6.2 Procedure for seeking permission

Permission must first be sought from the RPT concerned: LT rule 5C(1). If the RPT grants permission, notice of appeal must be given to the Registrar of the Lands Tribunal within 28 days of the grant of permission to appeal (LT rule 6(1)), except in cases where an urgency direction has been issued to reduce this time limit: LT rule 35A. An urgency direction may be issued upon application by a party or by the Tribunal acting on its own motion. There is power to extend the time limit for lodging the notice of appeal: LT rule 35, but no extension will be granted unless there is justification for it.

6.3 Forms for the notice of appeal can be obtained from the Tribunal. A completed form must be sent or delivered to the Tribunal together with a copy of the disputed decision and a copy of the RPT's decision granting permission to appeal.

6.4 If the RPT refuses permission to appeal, application for permission may be made to the Lands Tribunal within 14 days of the decision of the RPT to refuse permission: LT rule 5C(2). There is power to extend this time limit, (LT rule 35) but no extension will be granted unless there is justification for it.

6.5 Forms for the application can be obtained from the Lands Tribunal. These provide for the applicant to set out, in addition to their grounds of appeal, the reasons for the application for permission. It is for the applicant to satisfy the Tribunal that permission to appeal should be given and their reasons should therefore be set out fully as provided for on the form. The application must be accompanied by a copy of the decision against which permission to appeal is being sought and a copy of the decision of the RPT refusing permission to appeal.

6.7 If the Lands Tribunal grants permission, it may do so on such conditions as it thinks fit, including imposing conditions relating to costs. It is open to an appellant to undertake to pay all or part of a respondent's costs.

6.8 Approach of the Lands Tribunal to the grant of permission

On the application form applicants are asked to specify whether their reasons for making the application fall within one or more of the following categories:

  (a) the decision shows that the RPT wrongly interpreted or wrongly applied the relevant law.
  (b) The RPT took account of irrelevant considerations, or failed to take account of relevant consideration or evidence, or there was a substantial procedural defect.
  (c) The point or points at issue is or are of potentially wide implication.

6.9 The application must make clear whether the appellant is seeking

  (i)   an appeal by way of review, or
  (ii)   an appeal by way of review, which if successful will involve a consequential re-hearing, or
  (iii) an appeal by way of re-hearing.

Unless the application otherwise specifies, the application will be treated as an application for an appeal by way of review.

6.10 The Tribunal will grant permission to appeal only where it appears that there are reasonable grounds for concluding that the RPT may have been wrong for one or more of the reasons (a) to (c). In considering whether to grant permission on such grounds the importance of the point both to the decision itself and in terms of its wider implications will be a factor to be taken into consideration, in determining the proportionality and expedience of permitting an appeal to proceed. Where a successful appeal by review will necessitate a re-hearing, the Tribunal will have regard to the scope of such re-hearing in considering the proportionality of granting permission.

6.11 **Procedure on appeal**

The LT Rules Part III and Part VIII contain the procedure relating to appeals. Where an application for permission has been made and permission has been granted the application will be treated as the appellant's notice of appeal for the purposes of LT rule 6. Except in cases where the simplified procedure is followed under LT rule 28, the appellant will be required to serve a statement of case and each respondent will be required to serve a reply: see LT rule 8. Where a successful appeal by way of review will involve a consequential re-hearing of all or part of the evidence, unless the review is dealt with as a preliminary issue (see section 9 below), the review and the re-hearing will take place in the same hearing, and appropriate directions will be given for this purpose.

7. Urgency directions

7.1 For appeals from the LVT or the RPT an urgency direction may be issued to shorten the time limits that otherwise apply to the following actions:

(a) giving notice to the Registrar of the Lands Tribunal of an intention to appeal when permission to appeal has been granted by the LVT or the RPT: LT rule 6(1B);
(b) filing and serving a notice of intention to respond: LT rule 7(2B);
(c) filing and serving a statement of case: LT rule 8 (4B); or
(d) filing and serving a reply to a statement of case: LT rule 8(4B).

Any urgency direction may also permit the application to the LVT or to the RPT for permission to appeal to stand as notice to the Registrar of the Land Tribunal of an intention to appeal: LT rule 6(1B)(b).

7.2 LT rule 35A sets out the procedure for urgency directions. An urgency direction may be made by the Tribunal acting on its own initiative or on application by a party: LT rule 35A(2). Where the Tribunal proposes making an urgency direction, it will give notice in writing to the parties setting out the proposed direction or directions and will invite written representations on the proposal from the parties: LT rule 35A(9). The Tribunal may set a time period within which any such representations are to be made: LT rule 35A(10).

7.3 LT rule 35A(4) to (8) applies to applications made by a party for an urgency direction (in place of LT rule 38). A written application must be made in which the title of the proceedings and the ground upon which the application is made are set out: LT rule 35A(4). Consents signed by or on behalf of all parties must accompany any application that is made with the consent of all parties: LT rule 35A(6). The Tribunal will give written notice to the other parties and invite written representations on the application, (LT rule 35A (7)) unless the Tribunal, having considered the grounds upon which the application is made, decides to refuse the application: LT rule 53A (8). The Tribunal may set a time period within which any such representations are to be made: LT rule 35A(10).

In reaching a decision the Tribunal will take all written representations into account: LT rule 35A(11). An urgency direction will not be made unless the Tribunal is satisfied that it is in the interests of justice to do so: LT rules 6(1B), 7(2B) and 8(4B).

8. Statement of case and reply

8.1 Under Part III of the LT Rules, which relates to appeals, there are requirements that the appellant must serve a statement of case and the respondent must serve a reply. In the case of references there is no such requirement, but a statement of case and a reply will often be the appropriate way of ensuring that the issues are identified as soon as possible. In references, therefore, the Registrar (under the standard procedure) or a Member (under the special procedure) will normally order these at an early stage.

9. Preliminary issues

9.1 LT rule 43 enables the Tribunal on the application of any party to proceedings to order any preliminary issue in the proceedings to be disposed of at a preliminary hearing. In appropriate circumstances the procedure may enable the proceedings to be concluded more expeditiously and expense to be saved, and parties are therefore encouraged to consider whether there are any issues in a case which can with advantage be dealt with in this way. For its part the Tribunal will draw the parties' attention to issues which in its view might usefully be determined under this procedure.

9.2 Issues which may appropriately be the subject of a preliminary determination may be of law or of fact. Determination of a preliminary issue may effectively dispose of the whole case. Where it would not do so, however, it may nevertheless reduce the issues in the case and thereby avoid the cost and delay associated with the disclosure and inspection of documents, the preparation and exchange of experts' reports and valuations, and the pre-trial preparation on the part of solicitors and counsel, which the issues eliminated would otherwise have involved. On the other hand to attempt to deal as a preliminary issue with a matter which is not in reality severable from other issues in the case can lead to delay and increased cost.

9.3 An application under rule LT rule 43 should set out with precision the point of law or other issue or issues to be decided. It should where appropriate be accompanied by a statement of agreed facts, and it should state whether in the view of the party making the application the issue can be decided on the basis of the statement of agreed facts or whether evidence will be required. If evidence is said to be needed the application should state what matters that evidence would cover. The application should state why, in the applicant's view, determination of the issue as a preliminary issue would be likely to enable the proceedings to be disposed of more expeditiously and/or at less expense.

9.4 In order to consider an application that there should be a determination under LT rule 43 the Tribunal may require that witness statements and documentary evidence should be filed. If it decides to order that the issue should be determined as a preliminary issue it will give directions as to the filing in advance of the hearing of any experts' reports, witness statements, documentary evidence and statement of agreed facts that appear to it to be required.

9.5 An application under LT rule 43 is not appropriate for the determination of matters of title to the benefit of restrictive covenants for the purpose of applications to the Tribunal to discharge or modify restrictions under section 84 of the Law of Property Act 1925. That section makes specific provision for the giving of directions by the Tribunal as to who may be admitted to oppose such an application to discharge or modify restrictions and for reference to the Court of questions relating to the land affected by the restriction, the construction and effect of the restriction, and who, if anyone, can enforce it. The Tribunal has a separate procedure for the exercise of this statutory jurisdiction.

10. Extensions of time

10.1 Under LT rule 38 any time limit within which, either as prescribed by the LT rules or as laid down in any order or direction, a party is required to do anything may be extended on application to the Registrar. In general, justification for any such extension will be required, and the Registrar, or the Member to whom the case has been allocated, will consider any such application having regard to the overriding objective. In certain types of case, notably section 84 applications and leasehold enfranchisement appeals, delay may have substantial adverse consequences for one of the parties and the Tribunal will seek to enforce strictly any time limits laid down if such consequences are likely to occur.

11. Arranging the hearing

11.1 Where a hearing date has not already been fixed, the parties will be consulted as soon as the case is considered ready (either for a full hearing or for the determination of a preliminary issue). The views of the parties will be sought as to the estimated length of the hearing, the appropriate venue and suitable dates. Whilst every effort will be made to accommodate the parties' choice of counsel, there can be no absolute right to be represented by a particular member of the Bar. If, due to chosen counsel's unavailability, unacceptable listing delays would occur, the appointment of alternative counsel may be necessary. Once the parties have been consulted, and suitable dates determined, the case will be formally set down for the hearing and the parties officially notified. After the hearing has been fixed in this way the Tribunal will not order a postponement, even though the parties are agreed that there should be one, unless very good reasons are made out.

12. Venue

12.1 All parties are offered the option of a hearing at the Tribunal's own courts in London, and it is often possible to arrange earlier dates there than in a provincial court and to accommodate larger cases more easily than elsewhere. Where, for reasons of cost, accessibility, or the convenience of the parties and their representatives, it is desirable for a case to be heard outside London, the preferences of the parties will be met as far as it is practicable to do so. However, due to pressure on court accommodation it may be necessary for the parties to travel to the nearest major city, and there may be a smaller choice of dates.

13. Negotiations, settlements and withdrawals

13.1 The Tribunal encourages continued negotiations between the parties prior to the hearing with the objective of settling some or all of the issues, but the fact that such negotiations may be in progress will not constitute the sort of exceptional circumstances that would justify a postponement of the hearing. The parties should let the Tribunal know if, as the result of negotiations or other circumstances, time estimates for the hearing change. Where settlement of the case is reached before the hearing, the parties' representatives should advise the Tribunal immediately so that the hearing arrangements may be cancelled. Similarly, where an appeal, reference or application is to be withdrawn (LT rule 45(1)) or application is made to dismiss the proceedings (LT rule 45(2)) after the hearing date has been fixed, the Tribunal should be advised at the earliest opportunity.

14. Documentation

14.1 In cases assigned to the special or standard procedures, unless the Tribunal directs otherwise, the parties should lodge with the Tribunal not less than 14 days prior to the hearing sufficient copies (for the number of Members sitting) of a fully paginated agreed trial bundle containing the following:

(a) expert witness reports, including all appendices, photographs and plans referred to;
(b) witness statements;
(c) all other documents to be relied upon;
(d) a statement of agreed facts and issues.

The advocates' skeleton arguments should be lodged not less than 7 days before the hearing. Photocopies of any cases relied on should be provided for the Tribunal.

14.2 Plans and photographs should be appropriately annotated and indexed. Plans should be in A4 or A3 format unless there is good reason to use some other size.

15. Evidence

15.1 Those giving evidence at a hearing, whether of fact or as expert witnesses, should provide a written statement verified by a statement of truth. The form of the statement of truth is as follows:

"I believe that the facts stated in this witness statement are true."

The form of the statement of truth by an expert witness is as follows:

"I believe that the facts stated in this witness statement are true and that the opinions expressed are correct."

15.2 Evidence is given on oath or affirmation. Expert witnesses should comply with the provisions of the following paragraphs of these Practice Directions. An expert's report will stand as the expert's witness statement unless the Tribunal directs otherwise. A witness statement will stand as the witness's evidence in chief, but a witness giving oral evidence may, with the consent of the Tribunal, (a) amplify his witness statement, and (b) give evidence on new matters which have arisen since the witness statement was served. Notice of any such additional evidence should where possible be given to the other party, and any failure to do so will be taken into account by the Tribunal in deciding whether to give consent to such evidence being given. Paragraph 16.7 refers to supplementary experts' reports.

16. Expert evidence
16.1 Introduction
LT rule 42 applies to expert witnesses and their evidence. The nature of the jurisdictions exercised by the Tribunal means that the Tribunal will be called upon to hear and evaluate the evidence of experts in most cases. Expert witnesses are defined as those qualified by training and experience in a particular subject or subjects to express an opinion. Most frequently the expert witness before the Tribunal will be a surveyor or valuer, but this Part applies equally to any witness whom it is proposed to call to give expert evidence.

16.2 Duty of the expert witness
It is the duty of an expert to help the Tribunal on matters within his expertise. This duty overrides any obligation to the person from whom he has received instructions or by whom he is paid. The evidence should be accurate and complete as to relevant fact, and should represent the honest and objective opinion of the witness. If a professional body has adopted a code of practice and professional conduct dealing with the giving of evidence, then the Tribunal will expect a Member of that body to comply with the provisions of the code in the preparation and presentation of his evidence.

16.3 Where more than one party intends to call expert evidence
Where more than one party is intending to call expert evidence in the same field, the experts should take steps before preparing or exchanging their reports to agree all matters of fact relevant to their reports, including the facts relating to any comparable transaction on which they propose to rely, any differences of fact, and any plans, documents or photographs on which they intend to rely in their reports.

16.4 Form and content of expert's report
An expert's report should be addressed to the Tribunal and not to the party from whom the expert has received his instructions. It should:

(a) give details of the expert's qualifications;

(b) give details of any literature or other material on which the expert has relied in making the report;

(c) say who carried out any inspection or investigations which the expert has used for the report and whether or not the investigations have been carried out under the expert's supervision;

(d) give the qualifications of the person who carried out any such inspection or investigations, and

(e) where there is a range of opinion on the matters dealt with in the report
   (i) summarise the range of opinion; and
   (ii) give reasons for his own opinion;

(f) contain a summary of the conclusions reached;

(g) contain a statement that the expert understands his duty to the Tribunal and has complied with that duty and

(h) contain a statement setting out the substance of all material instructions (whether written or oral). The statement should summarise the facts and instructions given to the expert which are material to the opinions expressed in the report or upon which those opinions are based.

16.5 The instructions referred to in sub-paragraph (h) above will not be privileged against disclosure but the Tribunal will not, in relation to those instructions—

(i) order disclosure of any specific document; or

(ii) permit any questioning in the Tribunal, other than by the party who instructed the expert,

unless it is satisfied that there are reasonable grounds to consider the statement of instructions given under sub-paragraph (h) to be inaccurate or incomplete.

16.6 An expert's report should be verified by a statement of truth as well as the statements required by 16.4(g) and (h). Members of the Royal Institution of Chartered Surveyors should comply with the form of declaration contained in "Surveyors Acting as Expert Witnesses—Practice Statement" issued by the RICS. The form of the statement of truth is set out in paragraph 15.1 above.

16.7 **Lodging reports**

The procedures of the Tribunal are designed to ensure that all cases are disposed of speedily, efficiently and fairly. The role of the expert witness in these procedures is of fundamental importance. The directions given by the Tribunal will normally require the lodging and exchange of experts' reports and valuations at an early stage prior to the hearing. It is incumbent on the expert witness to prepare and submit such a report together with any valuation and details of comparable properties or transactions relied upon, fully and promptly for the purpose of lodging and exchange. Subject to paragraph 15.2 expert evidence given at the hearing will be confined to those matters disclosed in the expert's report. An expert who wishes to respond to the report of another expert should do so in a supplementary report, which will be treated as notice of additional evidence for the purposes of paragraph 15.2. Experts' reports must not contain any reference to or details of negotiations "without prejudice" or offers of settlement.

16.8 **Written questions to experts**

The Tribunal encourages parties to adopt the following procedure. Where they think it necessary to do so, a party should put written questions about their report to an expert instructed by another party. Normally such questions should be put once only; should be put within 28 days of service of the expert's report; and should be only for the purposes of clarification of the report. Where a party sends a written question or questions direct to an expert and the other party is represented by solicitors, a copy of the questions should, at the same time, be sent to those solicitors. It is for the party or parties instructing the expert to pay any fees charged by that expert for answering questions put under this procedure. This does not affect any decision of the Tribunal as to which party is ultimately to bear the expert's costs. An expert's answers to questions put in accordance with this paragraph will be treated as part of the expert's report.

16.9 Where a party has put a written question to an expert instructed by another party in accordance with the above paragraph, the Tribunal or the Registrar may order that the question must be answered; and the Tribunal may also make such an order in relation to a question that has not been put in this way. If the question is not answered the Tribunal or the Registrar may make one or both of the following orders in relation to the party who instructed the expert—

   (i) that the party may not rely on the evidence of that expert; or

   (ii) that the party may not recover the fees and expenses of that expert from any other party.

16.10 Where a party has disclosed an expert's report, any party may use that expert's report as evidence at the hearing.

16.11 **Discussions between experts**

After the exchange of the experts' reports the Tribunal will normally require experts of like discipline to meet in order to reach agreement as to facts, to agree any relevant plans, photographs, etc, to identify the issues in the proceedings and, where possible, to reach agreement on an issue. The Tribunal may specify the issues which the experts must discuss. The Tribunal may also direct that following a discussion between the experts the parties must prepare a statement for the Tribunal showing those facts and issues on which the experts agree and those facts and issues on which they disagree and a summary of their reasons for disagreeing. The Tribunal will usually regard failure to co-operate in reaching agreement as to the facts and issues as incompatible with the expert's duty to the Tribunal and may reflect this in any order on costs that it may make.

16.12 The contents of the discussions between the experts are not to be referred to at the hearing unless the parties agree. Where experts reach agreement on an issue during their discussions, the agreement will not bind the parties unless the parties expressly agree to be bound by the agreement.

16.13 Computer-based valuations

Where valuers propose to rely on computer-based valuations it is of the utmost importance that they should agree to employ a common model which can be made available for use by the Tribunal in the preparation of its decision. Directions should be sought from the Tribunal at an early stage if there is difficulty in reaching agreement.

17. Representation

17.1 At the hearing a party may appear and be heard in person (although a valuation officer may only do so with permission of the Tribunal), or may be represented by a barrister or a solicitor or, on obtaining permission from the Tribunal, by any other person (LT rule 37). A legal executive who is a Fellow of the Institute of Legal Executives and has a certificate covering the Lands Tribunal will be granted permission to represent his or her client, on application made at or prior to the hearing. An application for permission for a friend to represent a party who is an individual, or for one spouse to represent the other, will readily be granted and may be made at the hearing. Otherwise applications for permission to represent a party should be made in good time prior to the hearing, but the Tribunal may grant permission at the hearing as a matter of discretion. In simple cases, permission will usually be granted for a surveyor or valuer to represent a party in order to avoid the additional costs of separate representation. In those cases allocated to the simplified procedure under LT rule 28, such representation may well be the norm. In general, however, it is difficult and undesirable for the same person to act both as advocate and expert witness. Accordingly, permission will not be granted for a non-lawyer to represent a party in any case where the Tribunal considers that the responsibilities of advocate and of expert witness are likely to conflict.

18. Procedure at the hearing

18.1 The procedure at a hearing of the Tribunal is within the discretion of the presiding Member. The Tribunal is a court of law, and the procedure adopted will generally accord with the practice in the High Court and the county courts. In particular, the claimant, applicant or appellant will begin and will have a right of reply; evidence will be taken on oath, and the rules of evidence will be applied. The Tribunal will throughout seek to adopt a procedure that is proportionate, expeditious and fair in accordance with the overriding objective.

18.2 All cases assigned to the simplified procedure list will be heard by a single Member acting as if he were an arbitrator under LT rule 28. That LT rule and paras 3.3 and 3.4 of these Practice Directions should be referred to for further guidance to procedure in these cases.

18.3 The effect of LT rule 5 is that hearings by the Tribunal take place in public save in certain rare cases, principally where the Tribunal is sitting as an arbitrator under a reference by consent.

19. Site inspections

19.1 Where appropriate, the Tribunal may enter and inspect the land or property that is the subject of the proceedings, and, where practicable, any other land or properties referred to by the parties or their experts (LT rule 29). At such inspection, the Tribunal will (unless otherwise agreed) be accompanied by one representative from each side and will not accept any oral or written evidence tendered in the course of the inspection. The Tribunal may make an unaccompanied inspection without entering on private land.

20. Delivery of decisions

20.1 The Tribunal's decision will in most cases be reserved and will be in writing. LT rule 50(2) enables the Tribunal to give an oral decision at the end of the hearing, but this course is not normally appropriate.

21. Fees

21.1 The fees to be paid in respect of proceedings in the Lands Tribunal are specified in the Lands Tribunal (Fees) Rules 1996. Under the Lands Tribunal (Fees) (Amendment) Rules 2002 the Tribunal has power to reduce or remit fees in the case of hardship. Unless the Tribunal directs otherwise, the appropriate hearing fee is payable by the party initiating proceedings, but without prejudice to any right to recover the fee under an order for costs. A solicitor acting for a party must be on the record, and he will be responsible for the fees payable by that party while he is on the record (LT rule 53).

22. Costs

22.1 Under section 3(5) of the Lands Tribunal Act 1949 the Tribunal has power to order that the costs of any proceedings incurred by one party shall be paid by any other party. This power is limited by section 175(6) and (7) of the Commonhold and Leasehold Reform Act 2002 in the case of appeals from (see para 22.5 below). In awarding costs the Tribunal may settle the amount summarily or direct that they be the subject of detailed assessment by the Registrar on a specified basis.

22.2 Costs are in the discretion of the Tribunal, although this discretion is qualified by particular provisions in section 4 of the Land Compensation Act 1961 (see below para 22.3) and where the case is heard under the simplified procedure (see para 22.9 below). Subject to what is said below the discretion will usually be exercised in accordance with the principles applied in the High Court and county courts. Accordingly, the Tribunal will have regard to all the circumstances, including the conduct of the parties; whether a party has succeeded on part of his case, even if he has not been wholly successful; and admissible offers to settle (see paras 22.3 and 22.6 below). The conduct of a party will include conduct during and before the proceedings; whether a party has acted reasonably in pursuing or contesting an issue; the manner in which a party has conducted his case; and whether or not he has exaggerated his claim.

22.3 The general rule is that the successful party ought to receive his costs. On a claim for compensation for compulsory acquisition of land, the costs incurred by a claimant in establishing the amount of disputed compensation are properly to be seen as part of the expense that is imposed on him by the acquisition. The Tribunal will, therefore, normally make an order for costs in favour of a claimant who receives an award of compensation unless there are special reasons for not doing so. Particular rules, however, apply by virtue of section 4 of the Land Compensation Act 1961. Under this provision, where an acquiring authority have made an unconditional offer in writing of compensation and the sum awarded does not exceed the sum offered, the Tribunal must, in the absence of special reasons, order the claimant to bear his own costs thereafter and to pay the post-offer costs of the acquiring authority. However, a claimant will not be entitled to his costs if he has failed to deliver to the authority, in time to enable them to make a proper offer, a notice of claim containing the particulars set out in section 4(2). Where a claimant has delivered a claim containing the required details and has made an unconditional offer in writing to accept a particular sum, if the Tribunal's award is equal to or exceeds that sum the Tribunal must, in the absence of special reasons, order the authority to bear their costs and to pay the claimant's post-offer costs.

22.4 On an application to discharge or modify a restrictive covenant the general rule as to costs does not apply. The nature of proceedings under section 84 of the Law of Property Act 1925 is that the applicant is seeking to have removed from the objector particular property rights that the objector has. In view of this (and subject to any offer to settle that either party may have made), an unsuccessful objector who had the benefit of the covenant which has been discharged or modified will not normally have to pay any part of the applicant's costs unless he has acted unreasonably, and a successful objector will normally get all his costs unless he has in some respect been unreasonable.

22.5 On an appeal the Tribunal may not order a party to the appeal to pay costs incurred by another party unless he or she has, in the opinion of the Tribunal, acted frivolously, vexatiously, abusively, disruptively or otherwise unreasonably in connection with the appeal; and where, in view of such conduct, it does order a party to pay costs it may not award more than the LVT could order in such circumstances (currently £500).

22.6 In any proceedings a party may make an offer marked "without prejudice save as to costs" or similar wording (usually referred to as a *Calderbank* offer) in respect of the subject-matter of the appeal, application or reference. It may state a period within which it will remain open for acceptance but in order to protect the offeror fully it must be unconditional in point of time. Where an offer is accepted, the Tribunal retains jurisdiction over the costs of the proceedings except to the extent that these are covered by the agreed terms.

22.7 Where an offer has been made, the party making it may send a copy of it in a sealed cover to the Registrar or may deliver it at the hearing (see LT rule 44). The Tribunal will open the sealed offer after it has given its decision in the proceedings.

22.8 In a simple case or on an interlocutory hearing the Tribunal may make a summary assessment of costs. A party who proposes to apply for a summary assessment should prepare a summary of the costs and should serve it in advance on the other party. Costs which are to be the subject of a detailed assessment are referred to the Registrar under LT rule 52. The Tribunal will normally award costs on the standard basis. On this basis, costs will only be allowed to the extent that they are reasonable and proportionate to the matters in issue, and any doubt as to whether costs were reasonably incurred or reasonable and proportionate in amount will be resolved in favour of the paying party. Exceptionally the Tribunal may award costs on the indemnity basis. On this basis, the receiving party will receive all his costs except for those which have been unreasonably incurred or which are unreasonable in amount; and any doubt as to whether the costs were reasonably incurred or are reasonable in amount will be resolved in favour of the receiving party. A party who is dissatisfied with the Registrar's assessment of costs may apply to him for a review and, if still dissatisfied, he may apply to the President for a further review.

22.9 Where proceedings are determined in accordance with the simplified procedure under LT rule 28, costs will only be awarded where an offer to settle has been made and the Tribunal considers it appropriate to have regard to this offer, or the circumstances are exceptional. Where a case is determined in accordance with the written representations procedure under LT rule 27 costs are awarded in the usual way and not on the restricted basis of LT rule 28.

22.10 Where, as is almost invariably the case, the Tribunal issues a written decision determining the substantive issues in the proceedings, this will be sent to the parties with an invitation to make written submissions as to costs. Following consideration of these submissions the Tribunal will issue an addendum to the decision determining the liability for costs. It may be possible, particularly where there are only two possible outcomes of the proceedings, for the Tribunal to invite submissions as to costs at the conclusion of the hearing. This procedure will be followed wherever possible. Where the issue of costs is particularly complicated the Tribunal may hold a costs hearing before making an award.

23. Appeals to the Court of Appeal

23.1 Under section 3(4) of the Tribunal Act 1949 appeal lies to the Court of Appeal from a decision of the Tribunal. Appeal may be made on a point of law only. Previously the procedure required the Tribunal to state a case; but now, by virtue of the Civil Procedure (Modification of Enactment) Order 2000 (SI 2000 941), the procedure is that provided for by the Civil Procedure Rules. Under the CPR there is no longer a requirement for the Tribunal to state a case. Permission to appeal is required from the Court of Appeal. This must be requested in the appellant's notice (CPR rule 52.4(1)), and the appellant must file the appellant's notice at the Court of Appeal within 28 days after the date of the decision of the Tribunal (CPR Practice Direction to Part 52, paragraph 21.9). The decision of the Tribunal takes effect for this purpose on the day on which it is given unless the decision states otherwise; and usually the decision will state that it will take effect when, and not before, the issue of costs has been determined.

George Bartlett Q.C., President
Dated 11 May 2006

APPENDIX 2O

Leasehold Valuation Tribunals (Procedure) (England) Regulations 2003[136A]

(SI 2003/2099)

Citation, commencement and application
1169 Substitute for paragraph (3)(a)—

[(a) in the case of an application—

(i) of the description specified in paragraph 2(a) of Schedule 1, 31st October 2003;

(ii) of the description specified in paragraph 8 of that Schedule, 28th February 2005; and][136B]

New Footnote 136A: The Leasehold Valuation Tribunals (Procedure) (Amendment) (England) Regulations 2004 (SI 2004/3098) amend the 2003 Regulations as they apply in England. Different amendments in respect of Wales are included in Appendix 2X, below.
New Footnote 136B: Substituted by SI 2004/3098.

Particulars of applications
1170 Substitute for line 1 of paragraph 3—
[(3) Where an application is of a description specified in any of sub-paragraphs (b) to (f) of paragraph 2][136C]

1172 Insert after paragraph (7)
[(7A) Where an application is of the description specified in paragraph 8 of Schedule 1 (determination as to breach of covenant or condition) the particulars and documents listed in paragraph 7 of Schedule 2 shall be included with the application.][136D]

New Footnote 136C: Words substituted by SI 2004/3098.
New Footnote 136D: Added by SI 2004/3098 in force from February 28, 2005.

Determination without a hearing
1176 In reg 13(1) substitute the following for sub-paras (a) to (c):
[(4) Where an inspection is to be made, the tribunal shall give notice to the parties.

(5) A notice under paragraph (4) shall—

(a) state the date, time and place of the inspection; and

(b) be given not less than 14 days before that date.][136E]

New Footnote 136E: Substituted by SI 2004/3098 in force from February 28, 2005.

Inspections
Substitute for paras (4) to (7) in Regulation 17   **1176**

[(4) Where an inspection is to be made, the tribunal shall give notice to the parties.

(5) A notice under paragraph (4) shall—

(a) state the date, time and place of the inspection; and

(b) be given not less than 14 days before that date.][136F]

New Footnote 136F: Substituted by SI 2004/3098, in force from February 28, 2005.

Decisions
Replace Regulation 18(9) with the following: **1180**

(9) A copy of any document recording a decision, or the reasons for a decision, and a copy of any correction certified under paragraph (7) shall be sent to each party.

SCHEDULE 2

PARTICULARS OF APPLICATIONS

Enfranchisement and extended leases
Insert after sub-para (5):   **1183**

[(6) Except where an application is made under section 24, 25 or 27 of the 1993 Act, a copy of the lease.][136G]

New Footnote 136G: Added by SI 2004/3098, in force from February 28, 2005.

Estate management charges
Replace Schedule 2, paragraph 3(2)(b) with the following: **1183**

(b) a representative body within the meaning of section 71(3) of the 1993 Act; or

APPENDIX 2P

Heading should read:

1185   **Civil Procedure Rules 1998**

APPENDIX 2Q

Replace with the November 2006 Land Registry Practice Guide 27:   **1190**

1 Abbreviations and terms used

This guide deals with the relevant legislation contained in:

—the Leasehold Reform Act 1967, as amended by the Commonhold and Leasehold Reform Act 2002 (1967 Act);

—the Leasehold Reform, Housing and Urban Development Act 1993, as amended by the Commonhold and Leasehold Reform Act 2002 (1993 Act);

—the Landlord and Tenant Act 1987 (1987 Act);

—the Land Registration Act 2002 (LRA 2002);

—the Land Registration Rules 2003 (LRR 2003);

—the Land Registration (Amendment) (No.2) Rules 2005.

In this guide:

—"conveyancer" means a solicitor, a licensed conveyancer within the meaning of s. 11(2), Administration of Justice Act 1985, a Fellow of the Institute of Legal Executives (r.217(c), LRR 2003) or a duly certificated notary public (r.217(d), LRR 2003);

—"CRE" followed by a number means a Land Registry computerised register entry code;

—"prescribed clauses lease" means any lease, granted on or after 19 June 2006, which is required by r.58A of the LRR 2003 to contain the prescribed clauses set out in Schedule 1A to the LRR 2003.

2 Scope and further information

Note that the following are outside the scope of this guide.

—The amendments and provisions of the Commonhold and Leasehold Reform Act 2002 not in force at 1 May 2003.

—The extension of leases by agreement—see Practice Guide *28—Extension of leases*.

—The enfranchisement of places of worship under the Places of Worship (Enfranchisement) Act 1920.

—Deeds of enlargement under section 153 of the Law of Property Act 1925. In relation to leasehold enfranchisement and extension of leases of houses and flats, the Department for Communities and Local Government and the Welsh Assembly Government publish booklets covering various aspects of the legislation and procedures for exercising rights.

Land Registry publishes a range of guides. Some are referred to in the relevant sections. The following contain information relevant to a variety of applications covered by this guide and should be consulted as necessary.

—Practice Guide *19—Notices, restrictions and the protection of third party interests in the register* gives more detailed information on applications for the entry and removal of these entries.

—Practice Guide *46—Land Registry forms* gives details of the forms that must be used for various applications.

—Practice Guide *64—Prescribed clauses leases* gives more detailed information about prescribed clauses leases.

These can be obtained free of charge from any Land Registry office, or you can download them from our website.

3 Fees

Calculate fees in accordance with the current Land Registration Fee Order.

4 Preliminaries

4.1 Search of the index map

A tenant interested in acquiring the freehold reversion of their property or extending their lease should discover at the outset whether the title to the reversionary interest, or interests, is registered.

Do this by applying for an official search of the index map. The procedure is described in Practice Guide *10—Official searches of the index map*. It is inadvisable to apply for an official copy of the register without knowing the title number, as described in Practice Guide *11—Inspection and applications for official copies*, as this could result in an unwanted official copy being supplied.

The lessor's title number, if shown on the register of the applicant's title, is not always up to date. That title may of course be inspected—see section *4.2 Inspection of register of superior registered titles* but check the schedule of notices of leases carefully to ensure that it includes the applicant's lease. It is not enough to check the property register description as that too may be out of date if land has been removed from the title.

Land Registry Direct customers may be able to obtain all or some of the relevant title numbers by means of the property or postal description, but this is not a substitute for an official search of the index map.

4.2 Inspection of register of superior registered titles

Anyone may apply for an official copy of the entries on the register, the title plan and any documents referred to in the register that are kept by the registrar. These facilities are described in Practice Guide *11—Inspection and applications for official copies.*

5 Houses: enfranchisement and extension of leases under the Leasehold Reform Act 1967

5.1 Generally

The 1967 Act confers on a tenant of a house for the last two years under a long tenancy at a low rent the right to either:

—acquire, on enfranchisement, the freehold; *or*

—obtain an extended lease of the house and premises expiring 50 years after the date on which the existing term is due to expire—s.1AA of the 1967 Act (as amended).

There is an additional right to enfranchisement in relation to tenancies that fail the low rent test. "House" does not include flats in a horizontally divided building and "premises" includes any garage, outhouse, garden, yard and appurtenances, let and occupied, and used for the purpose of the house (s. 2(1) to (3) of the 1967 Act). "Long tenancy" means any tenancy originally granted for a term exceeding 21 years whether or not it is determinable by notice or re-entry (s. 3 of the 1967 Act (as amended)).

Business tenants of a house must meet a residency requirement and hold under a tenancy originally granted for 35 years or more.

The personal representatives of a deceased tenant now have limited rights of enfranchisement.

There are further conditions and exceptions that apply in particular circumstances.

Even if the original lease included the mines and minerals they will not be included in the enfranchisement if the landlord requires them to be excepted and provision is made for support of the property (s. 2(6) of the 1967 Act). A note of any exception will be entered in the register.

There are a variety of statutory provisions that apply to enfranchisement under the 1967 Act. If the deed or the application does not contain a clear statement, such as that set out below, the registrar will be unable to recognise it. There are a large number of applications to register the purchase of reversions and new leases entirely unconnected with the 1967 Act. If the applicant wishes to ensure that the application is completed quickly and accurately without requisitions:

—in the case of transfers, conveyances or other leases a statement along the following lines should appear prominently in the deed:

"This [transfer] [conveyance] [lease] is made under the provisions of the Leasehold Reform Act 1967.",
OR

—in the case of a prescribed clauses lease, clause LR5.2 should refer to the 1967 Act.

5.2 Protection of claims by notice

When a tenant has given notice of his desire to have the freehold or to have an extended lease, that notice may be protected as if it were an estate contract. If the reversionary title(s) affected are registered, this may be done by application for the entry of a notice under s. 34 of the LRA 2002. The tenant's right cannot constitute an interest that overrides within Schedules 1 or 3 to the LRA 2002. An application for an agreed notice should be made in form AN1 together with a certified copy of the notice (which will be filed at Land Registry). We will make the following entry in the charges register:

> *"Notice entered pursuant to section 5(5) of the Leasehold Reform Act 1967 that*
> *a notice dated _____ has been served under that Act by _____ of*
>
> _____
>
> *NOTE: Copy filed."*

(There is no CRE for this entry.)

Alternatively, application may be made for a unilateral notice by applying in form UN1.

If any of the reversionary titles affected are unregistered, the notice may be protected by a class C(iv) entry at the Land Charges Department.

5.3 Enfranchisement

On completion of the acquisition of the freehold title, application should be made in the usual way for registration of the transfer, if the title is already registered, or for the first registration of the land, if it is not.

If the tenant's or any superior leasehold interest is to be merged in the freehold, a request for merger should be included in the application, as described in *Appendix 1 Merger of leases on acquisition of the freehold*.

Where a deed of substituted security transferring a legal charge on a merged lease to the freehold is lodged, the charge will normally be registered against the freehold title. If the charge is only to be noted, lodge form AN1 or UN1, depending on whether the application is for an agreed or a unilateral notice.

NB: Where two or more charges are being registered their priorities must be clearly apparent. The following special provisions apply on the acquisition of the freehold of the house and will be reflected on the register.

5.3.1 Rights and burdens passing under the 1967 Act

Section 10(2) of the 1967 Act provides that certain rights that affect the leasehold interest shall automatically continue on enfranchisement for and against the freehold but without prejudice to any rights that may be expressly granted or reserved.

The rights passing under s. 10(2) that take effect "so far as the landlord is capable of granting them" are rights of support, rights of access of light and air and rights to the passage, use or maintenance of the usual common services, such as water, gas or other piped fuel, drainage, electricity, telephone and so on.

Entries will always be made in the register in respect of the land transferred, whether or not the lease is merged:

In the property register

> *"The land _____ has the benefit of such easements and rights as the ____ dated _____ referred to in the Charges Register has had the effect of granting by virtue of section 10(2)(i) of the Leasehold Reform Act 1967____."*[142]

Or

> *"The land _____ has the benefit of such easements and rights as the _____ dated ____ referred to above has had the effect of granting by virtue of section 10(2)(i) of the Leasehold Reform Act 1967_____."*[143]

If the conveyance or transfer expressly excludes or restricts any of the appurtenant rights, which would otherwise be deemed to pass by statutory implication, this will be reflected at the end of the above entry.

In the charges register

> *"The land _____ is subject to such easements and rights as by a ____ dated _____ made between _____it was made subject to by virtue of section 10(2)(ii) of the Leasehold Reform Act 1967."*[144]

Or

> *"The land _____ is subject to such easements and rights as by the ____ dated_____ referred to above it was made subject to by virtue of section 10(2)(ii) of the Leasehold Reform Act 1967."*[145]

No reference will normally be made to any deed (whether it be the lease or otherwise) that contains a grant or reservation of rights granted by virtue of s. 10(2) of the 1967 Act. If, however, specific application is made, an entry will be made on the following lines:

> *"In relation to the effect of section 10(2)(i) [or (ii)] of the Leasehold Reform Act 1967 a lease/transfer/deed dated _____ made between _____ granted/ reserved the following rights [or rights of drainage, or as the case may be]."*

(There is no CRE for this entry.)

---

[142] CRE AK211 contains fields in the order *1*, *2*, *3*, *9*.
[143] CRE AK130 contains fields in the order *1*, *2*, *3*, *9*.
[144] CRE CK795 contains fields in the order *1*, *2*, *3*, *4*.
[145] CRE CK355 contains fields in the order *1*, *2*, *3*.

If the conveyance or transfer expressly excludes or restricts any of the appurtenant rights, which would otherwise be deemed to pass by statutory implication, an entry of this provision will be made in the property register. If the conveyance or transfer contains new easements or restrictive covenants under s. 10(3) and (4) of the 1967 Act, entries relating to them will be made in the register in accordance with normal practice.

Applicants should ensure that either:

—if the reversion over which the easement is granted is registered in the name of the landlord but under a different title to that of the house, application is also made against the servient title, or

—where the land is unregistered that good title is deduced.

Where a transfer of part of a registered title is made pursuant to the 1967 Act, the rights created under s. 10(2) will call for entries to be made on the transferor's title as well.

Where the transferor's title comprises no more than three properties, specific entries on the lines of those referred to above will be made, but where it comprises more properties an entry in the following terms will be made in the property register:

"Such transfers of the parts edged and numbered in green on the title plan as were made under the Leasehold Reform Act 1967 took effect with the benefit of and subject to easements and other rights as prescribed by section 10(2) of that Act."[146]

5.3.2 Discharge of charges on landlord's estate (whether registered or unregistered)

No difficulty will arise if any registered or noted charge, or any mortgage against the landlord's title, can be discharged or released in the normal way when the tenant acquires the freehold. However, the 1967 Act provides additional mechanisms for the discharges of charges or mortgages where necessary, which may mean that the conventional evidence or receipt may be inappropriate. The following paragraphs describe what evidence will be accepted in these cases:

—The purchasing tenant may have paid sufficient money to the landlord's mortgagee direct in order to discharge the land from the mortgage (s. 12 of the 1967 Act). If the mortgagee has accepted payment of the whole or a sufficient part of the purchase money in full discharge of the property from his mortgage, a copy of the receipt, so worded, must be lodged with the application.

—If the money has been paid into court under s. 13 of the 1967 Act, the tenant must supply a copy of the affidavit, which he will have made for that purpose, and also a copy of the court's official receipt.

---

[146] CRE AK164 contains no fields.

We may serve a notice after the application for registration has been lodged. The notice will be served on the registered mortgagee and any other party appearing by the register to have an interest in the mortgage, and will give details of:

—the mortgage

—the applicants and the nature of the application

—the intended closure of the relevant part of the title if the transfer is of part

—how any objection to the application can be made.

If no reply to the notice is received within the time allowed, registration will be completed free from any reference to the charge. If the mortgagee shows prima facie grounds for objection in reply to the notice (for example, because an insufficient part of the purchase money has been paid into court), it may be agreed that the entry of the mortgage will remain on the register of the purchaser's title until proper evidence of a full discharge is produced, or the matter is otherwise settled.

5.3.3 Landlord's estate subject to a rentcharge
The transfer or conveyance will normally take effect subject to any pre-existing rentcharges affecting the title.[147] However, where the rentcharge is more than the amount payable as rent under the lease, the tenant can require the landlord to discharge the house and premises from the rentcharge to the extent of the excess. Where difficulties arise in paying the redemption price, provision is made for payment into court (s. 11(4) of the 1967 Act). The evidence we require for the discharge of the rentcharge will be similar to that mentioned in section 5.3.2 *Discharge of charges on landlord's estate (whether registered or unregistered).*
    The landlord may either:

—procure a release of the rentcharge from the rentcharge owner. The normal conveyancing evidence will be required including the production of any relevant certificates; *or*

—require, subject to the reasonable consent of the tenant,[148] that the rentcharge shall be charged exclusively on other land so as to exonerate the land conveyed or else that it shall be apportioned. The normal conveyancing evidence of formal or informal exoneration or apportionment must be produced.

5.4 Extended leases
Because the 1967 Act allows individual leaseholders to acquire the freehold of their properties, few applications for registration of extended leases under that

---

[147] Subsections 8(2) and (4)(b) of the 1967 Act (as amended by the Rentcharges Act 1977, s. 17(1), Sch. 1, para. 4).
[148] Section 11(1) of the 1967 Act (as amended by the Rentcharges Act 1977, s. 17(1), Sch. 1, para. 4(2).

Act have been received. However, since the provisions are still available for use, and if used can create difficulties for us, applications for registration of such leases are dealt with in the following paragraphs.

5.4.1 Registration of new lease—Land Registry requirements
On completion of the acquisition of a new lease granted in substitution for an existing lease pursuant to s.14, 1967 Act, make an application for registration of the lease. If necessary, also lodge an application to give effect on the register to the deemed surrender of the existing lease, which will have taken place by operation of law.

Appendix 2—Applications for registration of extended leases explains Land Registry's requirements in connection with these applications.

5.4.2 Entries in the register
Where appropriate, the following entry will be made on the new title:

> *"The land is subject to such rights as may be subsisting in favour of the persons interested under a Charge dated _____ and made between _____of the leasehold interest under a Lease dated _____ in substitution of which, pursuant to the Leasehold Reform Act 1967, the registered lease was granted."*[149]

If it is not possible to make the type of entry described above (for example, because the original lease is unregistered and no evidence as to any mortgages affecting it has been produced), the following entry will be made:

> *"The land is subject to such rights as may be subsisting in favour of the persons interested under any charge of the leasehold interest under a Lease dated _____ in substitution for which pursuant to the Leasehold Reform Act 1967, the registered lease was granted."*[150]

5.5 Sub-leases
There are complicated provisions in Schedule 1 to the 1967 Act to determine which lessor is to act as reversioner on behalf of all the lessors where there are sub-leases.

It is important to note that the sub-lessee does not necessarily have to serve the notice under s. 5 to the 1967 Act on all persons interested (see para. 8 of Schedule 3 to the 1967 Act).

5.6 Miscellaneous

5.6.1 Consent by Charity Commissioners not required
Where the landlord's title is held by a charity then the transfer or lease will not be affected by any restriction in the register in form E to Schedule 4 to the LRR

---

[149] CRE CK889 contains fields in the order *3*, *4*, *3*.
[150] CRE CK179 contains field *3*.

2003. However, any disposition of registered or unregistered land must contain the appropriate statement and where the lease is a prescribed clauses lease, the statement must be included in clause LR5.1.

5.6.2 Rights of future development and pre-emption

On enfranchisement or extension of a lease, certain landlords, including local authorities and the Commission for the New Towns, may require the tenant to enter into:

—covenants to restrain the tenant from developing or clearing the land in case the lessor may need it for future development;

—a covenant that he will not grant a tenancy of the property without the consent of the landlord and that he will not sell it without first offering it to the landlord.

We will make an appropriate entry in the register if a conveyance, transfer, or extended lease contains covenants of this nature (paragraph 1(3) of Schedule 4 to the 1967 Act as amended).

6 Flats: enfranchisement and extension of leases of flats under the Leasehold Reform, Housing and Urban Development Act 1993

6.1 Generally

Part I of the 1993 Act gives qualifying tenants of flats either:

—a collective right to buy the freehold of the block (collective enfranchisement) if the flats are contained in premises that satisfy certain conditions; *or*

—an individual right to a new lease expiring 90 years after the termination of an existing lease.

Neither of these rights can be exercised when the National Trust owns any interest or when the flat is within the precinct of a cathedral. A precinct is defined under the Care of Cathedrals Measure 1990 by reference to the plans kept by the Cathedrals Fabric Commission for England. Where the Crown is not the immediate landlord but is a superior landlord, then, in some cases, there will be a right to a new lease (s. 94 of the 1993 Act).

6.2 Tenants' right to collective enfranchisement

6.2.1 Generally

This is the right of tenants to acquire the freehold of their block whether or not the landlord wishes to sell.

The 1993 Act lays down a framework within which negotiations take place with the aim of entering into a contract for sale in the normal way. The 1993 Act does not contain any provision for the grant of statutory easements, unlike the

1967 Act described in section *5 Houses: enfranchisement and extension of leases under the Leasehold Reform Act 1967*. Instead, the 1993 Act says that the parties must include, in the conveyance or transfer, any necessary easements, such as rights of support, so the parties have to decide what is required in their particular situation.

In acquiring the freehold any intermediate lease between the tenants' leases and the freehold is also acquired. The tenants will, therefore, hold their flat leases directly of the freeholder. This means that even if the tenants already have a flat management company holding an intermediate lease, that lease will be acquired under s. 2(1) of the 1993 Act. It would not appear that there is any way this can be avoided since s. 2(1)(a) and (2) appear to be mandatory. In these circumstances the tenants should perhaps consider not using the procedure in the 1993 Act.

Where tenants acquire the premises outside the legislation, by independent negotiation, the provisions of the 1993 Act do not apply.

It is, therefore, a requirement that the conveyance or transfer must contain a statement in the following terms where the 1993 Act procedure is used:

> *"This conveyance [or transfer] is executed for the purposes of Chapter I of Part I of the Leasehold Reform, Housing and Urban Development Act 1993."*[151]

Chapter I of Part I of the 1993 Act confers on qualifying tenants of flats the right to have the freehold of the premises, in which the flats are contained, acquired on their behalf by a person appointed by them for the purpose.

A person so appointed is known as the nominee purchaser (s. 1 of the 1993 Act).

A person is a qualifying tenant if he is a tenant under a long lease for a term exceeding 21 years.

6.2.2 Protection of tenants rights—notices

The procedures whereby qualifying tenants assert their collective rights to have the freehold acquired are outside the scope of this guide. See section *6.4 Notices* for the procedure for protecting a notice of claim to exercise such rights.

6.2.3 Completion of acquisition

When all matters have been agreed between the parties, or otherwise resolved, a binding contract is entered into for the acquisition of the freehold and superior leasehold interests by the nominee purchaser with the reversioner (s. 34(2) and paragraph 6(1)(b)(ii) of Schedule 1 to the 1993 Act). Precisely who is the reversioner may be complex, particularly where there are intermediate leasehold titles.

The acquisition is then completed by a conveyance or transfer of the freehold to the nominee purchaser, subject only to such incumbrances as may have been agreed or determined. The 1993 Act makes provision for the kind of matters that

---

[151] Section 34(10) of the 1993 Act and r.196 of the LRR 2003.

should be included in any sale, without being prescriptive as to their exact content. Where the purchase involves the acquisition of a superior leasehold interest, title will need to be deduced, if it is not registered, to all interests acquired, as will title to land over which any party grants easements in favour of the land acquired by the nominee purchaser. Where the leasehold or freehold interests, or any adjacent land over which easements are granted, are registered, application against the respective titles is required.

If the freeholder is granting easements and the land over which they are being granted is held in lease by a leaseholder, part of whose interest is also being sold to the nominee purchaser, for the easements to be effective as against that leaseholder the leaseholder will have to be a party to the grant of the freehold easements so that they are binding on it during the term of the lease.

This will involve an entry being made on the leaseholder's title so that subsequent owners will have notice of the rights.

The conveyance or transfer is effective to overreach any incumbrances that are capable of being overreached (s. 34(3) of the 1993 Act), which means most incumbrances that would be overreached on a sale at arm's length. The main exception is some rentcharges that are covered below. Mortgages on the freehold or intermediate titles are also discussed later.

The person who executes the transfer or conveyance will normally be the freeholder, whom the 1993 Act designates as the reversioner. Where there are intermediate leasehold titles the reversioner will act on behalf of the other landlords in the transfer or conveyance and execute the deed on their behalf, although they should be described as being parties to the deed for the purpose of the sale and any concurrence to the grant of easements or other rights (paragraph 6(1)(iii) of Schedule 1 to the 1993 Act). However, the other landlords can opt out of this procedure and can transfer or convey the interest themselves, as indeed can the nominee purchaser (paragraph 7 of Schedule 1 to the 1993 Act).

Where an intermediate leasehold title is unregistered, it would be advisable for a note of any transfer of part or grant of an easement to be endorsed on the lease.

The registrar will assume, where an intermediate landlord is described as party to the transfer, that no opt out has taken place. However, if the transfer is silent, a requisition will be raised requiring a separate transfer, conveyance or assignment of the intermediate interest.

Where the reversioner, being the person making the transfer to the nominee purchaser, is shown on the title as the registered proprietor of the freehold, or is shown as having the legal estate in fee simple absolute in an unregistered title, no further evidence as to the power of the reversioner to convey the block will be needed. Where, however, the court has appointed any other person to be the reversioner, a certified copy of the court order will be required. A person so appointed acts as if he was the freehold reversioner (Schedule 1, Part I to the 1993 Act).

6.2.4 Registration of nominee purchaser

The nominee purchaser can be any person or persons (which includes a company) appointed by the participating tenants. Although the 1993 Act calls the purchaser a "nominee" it may well be the case that they are not, in fact, a nominee at law. If a company or other body corporate is used as a vehicle to buy the land it seems likely that the company will be beneficially entitled with the qualifying tenants exercising their rights through their shareholding. Whether the nominee purchaser is a true nominee, or perhaps some other type of trustee, an application for a suitable restriction should accompany the application for registration of the nominee purchaser.

NB: The registrar will not enter a restriction unless one is applied for appropriately or the LRA 2002 or the LRR 2003 otherwise require it. In almost all cases, the existing tenants' leases will be incumbrances to which the sale is subject. Counterparts of these leases, and any new lease back, must be produced with the application if they are not already noted as incumbrances in the charges register of the title affected by the sale. Subject to the points mentioned in this section, the application should be made in the usual way in form AP1 or FR1 depending on whether the reversioner's title is registered or unregistered. Leasehold interests that merge should be dealt with in accordance with *Appendix 1—Merger of leases of acquisition of the freehold*.

6.2.5 Unpaid vendor's lien

A vendor's lien is capable of arising on the transfer to the nominee purchaser, where an amount remains outstanding in any of the following categories (s. 32(2) of the 1993 Act):

—The price payable;

—Amounts due from tenants (not just those who are participating in the purchase) in respect of their leases or under or in respect of agreements collateral thereto;

—Any amount payable to the vendor by virtue of s. 18(2) of the 1993 Act (where the valuation has been reduced by a failure of the nominee purchaser to reveal the existence of a relevant agreement or shareholding).

—Any costs payable by the nominee purchaser (s. 33 of the 1993 Act);

The lien is not capable of substantive registration, but can be the subject of an application for protection by way of notice in the register. However, since the lien does not arise automatically, but depends upon the circumstances of the particular case, we will take no action except on receipt of a specific application to note the lien.

6.2.6 Discharge of mortgages on the landlord's estate (and any leaseholder's estate that is being acquired) on transfer to the nominee purchaser (whether registered or unregistered)

It is preferable for any registered or noted charge or any mortgage against the landlord's title or any intermediate lessee's title to be discharged, cancelled or receipted in the normal way when the tenant acquires the freehold. This is because, despite the provisions of s. 35 of the 1993 Act referred to below, it will never be clear that its provisions apply, unless the money has been paid into court, because of the severely limiting effect of paragraph 2 of Schedule 8 to the 1993 Act (Duty of nominee purchaser to redeem mortgages).

Unless a form DS1, form DS3, Electronic Discharge, Electronic Notification of Discharge, application to cancel a notice, or evidence of payment into court is produced with the application the registrar will either requisition for a statutory declaration or serve notice, where possible, on the person having the benefit of the mortgage or charge.

The following describes what evidence will be satisfactory for our purposes and what action we will take.

Under the 1993 Act the transfer or conveyance has the effect of discharging all the land acquired, including any intermediate leasehold interest, from any charge on it (s. 35(1) of the 1993 Act) without the mortgagee or chargee having to execute the transfer or conveyance or becoming parties to the conveyance. The parties can, however, agree that the land will be subject to the mortgage. If the parties intend this to happen then the transfer or conveyance should make this absolutely clear, otherwise the charges may be cancelled.

The nominee purchaser may have paid sufficient money to the landlord's chargee direct in order to discharge the land from the charge. If the chargee has accepted payment of the whole, or a sufficient part of the purchase money, in full discharge of the property from the charge, a copy of the receipt must be lodged with the application.

If the money has been paid into court under s. 35 of, and Schedule 8 to, the 1993 Act, the purchaser must supply a copy of the affidavit which he will have made for that purpose, and also a copy of the court's official receipt. We may serve notice of the application on the registered chargee and any other person appearing by the register to be interested in the charge.

It will give details of:

—the charge;

—the applicants and the nature of the application;

—the intended closure of the relevant part of the title where it is a transfer of part;

—how any objection to the application can be made.

If no reply to the notice is received within the time allowed, registration will be completed free from any reference to the charge.

If the chargee shows prima facie grounds for objection in reply to the notice, for example, because an insufficient part of the purchase money has been paid into court, it may be agreed that the entry of the charge will remain on the register of the purchaser's title until proper evidence of a full discharge is produced or the matter is otherwise settled.

6.2.7 Landlord's estate subject to a rentcharge

The transfer or conveyance will normally take effect subject to any pre-existing rentcharge affecting the title (s. 34(6) of the 1993 Act). The landlord may either:

—procure a release of the rentcharge from the rentcharge owner. The normal conveyancing evidence will be required; *or*

—require, subject to the reasonable consent of the tenant (s. 34(8) of the 1993 Act),

that the rentcharge shall be charged exclusively on other land so as to exonerate the land conveyed or else that it shall be apportioned. The normal conveyancing evidence of formal or informal exoneration or apportionment must be produced.

6.2.8 Lease back to the former freeholder

On acquiring the freehold in the whole of the building the nominee purchaser is required in certain circumstances to grant leases back to the former freeholder of those units or flats in the building not leased by the qualifying tenants and which they are not acquiring. Such leases will be for terms of 999 years at a peppercorn rent (s. 36 of, and Schedule 9 to, the 1993 Act).

The application for registration of such a lease must be made in form AP1 or FR1 depending on whether the reversioner's title is registered. Furthermore, the position with regard to the status of the lease will differ depending on whether or not the freehold is already registered.

Registered freehold

The new lease will be a disposition of registered land and will, therefore, take effect in equity only until registered. It would seem that the potential lessee is a purchaser within the meaning of r.131 of the LRR 2003 in order to be able to make a protecting search. Since the 1993 Act provides that the nominee purchaser must grant the lease back, the transaction is one where any contemporaneous mortgagee of the freehold will be subject to the right to a new lease. An official search will secure the priority to which the intended lessee is entitled.

The lessee should also make the nature of the transaction clear in a letter accompanying the application for registration.

This is because since the lessee has no control over the timing of the application for registration of the freehold disposal, it is possible that the application for registration of the lease will be made before that of the freehold. It will then appear that the freeholder is attempting to grant a lease to himself, which is not possible, and we would reject the application. Where this "mistiming" occurs we will hold the leasehold application, but when we receive the application for the freehold transfer it will be entered on the day list of pending applications and the leasehold application will then be reentered on the day list after the transfer so that the priorities are correct.

Unregistered land

Where the freehold is unregistered it will be subject to first registration and the new lease will take effect as a legal estate whether or not the purchaser makes the application for registration before the new lease application is lodged. Again, it would be helpful if there could be an accompanying letter setting out the circumstances. When the freehold application is lodged the application should reveal the existence of the lease back and the counterpart should be lodged with the application.

The usual conveyancing evidence of the freehold title will be required, including the appropriate Land Charges searches.

6.2.9 Vesting orders

Chapter I of Part I, 1993 Act gives power to the court to make vesting orders where:

—the terms of acquisition are in dispute;

—there is a failure to enter into a contract (s. 24 of the 1993 Act); *or*

—the reversioner fails to give a counter-notice (s. 25 of the 1993 Act) or cannot be found or identified (s. 26 of the 1993 Act).

As to the protection of such orders see sections *6.4.2 Vesting orders made under ss. 26(1) or 50(1) of the 1993 Act (where the relevant landlord cannot be found or identified)* and *6.4.3 Orders made under ss. 24, 25, 48 or 49 of the 1993 Act (where there is a dispute)*.

6.2.10 Variation of flat leases

Nothing in the collective enfranchisement procedure has any effect on the length of the tenants' leases. Where the tenants wish to take advantage of their new found freedom to 'extend' their leases they may do so by agreement, or possibly by exercising rights under Chapter II of Part I of the 1993 Act. They should, however, be aware of the traps the law contains in this area and note Land Registry's requirements in connection with the voluntary extension of leases as set out in Practice Guide *28—Extension of leases*. You can obtain this from any Land Registry office or download it from our website.

6.3 Right of a tenant to acquire a new lease

Chapter II of Part I, 1993 Act confers on a qualifying tenant of a flat for the last two years an individual right to acquire a new lease of the flat on payment of a premium determined in accordance with a statutory formula.

NB: A person is a qualifying tenant if they are (subject to certain exceptions) a tenant under a long lease of a flat (s. 39(3) of the 1993 Act). The right is suspended if the tenants collectively seek to buy the freehold.

6.3.1 Procedure on tenant's claim to new lease

The procedures whereby a qualifying tenant asserts their claim to a new lease are beyond the scope of this guide except that the procedure for protecting a notice of claim to exercise such a right is discussed in section *6.4 Notices*.

6.3.2 Terms of the new lease

The new lease, which takes effect in substitution for the existing lease, will be for a term expiring 90 years after the term date of the existing lease at the rent of a peppercorn (s. 56(1) of the 1993 Act). The new lease is to be on the same terms as the existing lease but with such modifications as may be required or appropriate (s. 57 of the 1993 Act).

Although the right is a right to have a new lease of the land demised to the tenant, under the existing lease it is clear that variations in extent and in the rights granted are permitted (s. 57(1) of the 1993 Act). Very careful examination of the extents of any existing flats and of the terms of easements will, therefore, be required to ensure that the landlord has power to grant the new lease. It is quite likely that some new leases will not be of the same extent since over a long period there are informal arrangements between tenants that 'vary' the terms of their leases in practice. This may cause problems on the grant of new leases, for example the switching of use of car parking spaces, dustbin areas and other common facilities. Landlords will need to ensure that the extent granted and the terms of the new lease (including any easements) are compatible with any other leases that exist.

6.3.3 Statement to be contained in new lease

The lease must contain a statement in the following terms:

> "This lease is granted under section 56 of the Leasehold Reform, Housing and Urban Development Act 1993." (s. 57(11) of the 1993 Act and r.196 of the LRR 2003).

Where the lease is a prescribed clauses lease this statement must be inserted in clause LR5.1 or reference made to the clause, paragraph or schedule in the lease that contains this statement in full.

If the lease does not contain such a statement the registrar will assume that it is not made pursuant to the 1993 Act. Although there is no prescribed form of statement where the lease is granted under s. 93(4) of the 1993 Act (leases granted on terms approved by the court) it would be helpful if it did contain such a statement because of the consequences that flow from that section as mentioned in the following paragraphs. In those circumstances a certified copy of the court order under that section should also be produced.

6.3.4 Reversionary titles

If the qualifying tenant's immediate landlord does not have a sufficient interest (ie is not the freeholder and does not have a leasehold interest of sufficient duration to enable such landlord to grant a new lease) then the new lease will be granted by the nearest landlord whose interest is sufficient, and he will be the 'competent landlord' for the purposes of the 1993 Act (s. 40(1) and (2) of the 1993 Act). The intermediate landlord's title may be registered but the competent landlord's title unregistered.

The early identification of the competent landlord is important in order to determine what evidence of his title to grant the lease is required (see *Appendix 2—Applications for registration of extended leases*).

This raises certain problems in relation to an existing intermediate lease.

The competent landlord's title

The new lease will be a disposition by the competent landlord. If the competent landlord's title is registered, the following note will be made in the schedule of notice of leases.

> *"NOTE: The lease was made under the provisions of section 56 or 93(4) of the Leasehold Reform, Housing and Urban Development Act 1993."* (There is no CRE for this entry.)

If a lease that includes the flat is noted on the competent landlord's title then an additional entry will be made against it along the following lines.

> *"The lease dated _____ to _____ [referred to above] was deemed to have been surrendered and regranted following the grant of a lease or leases under section 56 or 93(4) of the Leasehold Reform, Housing and Urban Development Act 1993 with the effect provided for by paragraph 10 of Schedule 11 to that Act."* (There is no CRE for this entry.)

Applicants and their advisers will need to consider what conveyancing evidence and memoranda, if any, should be endorsed on or placed with the deeds.

Intermediate leasehold title(s)

The 1993 Act makes special provision for the situation where there are intermediate leases (s. 40(3) of, and Schedule 11 to, the 1993 Act).

An intermediate lessor has a reversionary interest which does not have enough years left to grant a new lease. There may be more than one intermediate lessor. The right to grant the new lease is vested only in the competent landlord but the 1993 Act provides that any intermediate lease is deemed to have been surrendered and regranted. This is a device to ensure that the integrity of intermediate leases of the whole block and any service charge arrangements contained in them are preserved. The registrar has concluded that this provision does not have the effect of actually effecting a surrender and regrant that would require intermediate lessees to apply for the closure of their title and an application to register it again. The intermediate lessor is bound by the terms of the new lease as it is granted pursuant to a statutory power. Notice that the new lease has been registered should be served on any registered intermediate lessor.

An entry will be made in the property register along the following lines:

> *"The registered lease is deemed to have been surrendered and regranted following the grant of a lease or leases under section 56 or 93(4) of the Leasehold Reform, Housing and Urban Development Act 1993 with the*

effect specified in paragraph 10 of Schedule 11 to that Act." (There is no CRE for this entry.)

Any lease granted under these provisions will be noted in the schedule of notice of leases and a note to the entry will be made along the following lines:

> *"NOTE: This lease was granted under the provisions of section 56 or 93(4) of the Leasehold Reform, Housing and Urban Development Act 1993 and the provisions of paragraph 10 of Schedule 11 to that Act apply."* (There is no CRE for this entry.)

The only circumstance where these provisions in relation to intermediate leases do not apply is where an intermediate lease is owned by the tenant or is held on trust for him (paragraph 10(3) of Schedule 11 to the 1993 Act). Where this is the case the tenant's application will need to make this clear and include an application to close (perhaps as to part) any registered title affected, since the effect of the grant of the new lease is to bring about the immediate surrender of the intermediate lease.

6.3.5 Registration of new lease—Land Registry requirements
When a new lease is acquired in substitution for an existing lease, pursuant to s. 56 of the 1993 Act, make an application for registration of the lease. If necessary also lodge an application to give effect to the deemed surrender of the existing lease, which will have taken place by operation of law. *Appendix 2—Application for registration of extended leases* explains our requirements in connection with these applications.

6.3.6 Entries in the register
The following entry will be made in the property register immediately after the entry relating to the registered lease:

> *"The registered lease was granted under the provisions of section 56 or 93(4) of the Leasehold Reform, Housing and Urban Development Act 1993."* (There is no CRE for this entry.)

The reason for this entry is that under s. 56 of the 1993 Act, if the registered proprietor grants a new long lease out of the title, the subtenant has no right to claim a new lease from the competent landlord under that Act.

Where a charge is brought forward from the surrendered leasehold estate, its date of registration will be that of the application to register the new lease. The following entry will be made on the registration or re-registration of the charge:

> *"This charge, [which] takes effect against this title under the provisions of section 58(4) of the Leasehold Reform, Housing and Urban Development Act 1993, [was formerly registered against title number(s)_____]"* (There is no CRE for this entry.)

If the charge is merely being noted, there will be an entry on similar lines:

"This charge, [which] takes effect against this title under the provisions of section 58(4) of the Leasehold Reform, Housing and Urban Development Act 1993, [was formerly noted against title number(s)_____]" (There is no CRE for this entry.)

Unless postponed, all charges and other entries brought forward will have the same priority as they had on the old title.[152]

6.3.7 Possession of lease and certificate where mortgagee held deeds of surrendered lease

Where a new lease takes effect, subject to a mortgage and the mortgagee is at that time entitled to possession of title documents relating to the surrendered lease, the mortgagee becomes similarly entitled to possession of the documents of title relating to the new lease. In such a case, the tenant is bound to deliver the new lease to the mortgagee within one month of the date on which it is received from Land Registry following its registration.

6.3.8 Vesting orders

The court has power to make vesting orders where the terms of acquisition are in dispute or there is failure to enter into a lease (s. 48 of the 1993 Act) or where the reversioner fails to give a counter-notice (s. 49 of the 1993 Act) or cannot be found or identified (s. 50 of the 1993 Act). As to the protection of such orders see sections *6.4.2 Vesting orders made under s. 26(1) or 50(1) of the 1993 Act* and *6.4.3 Orders made under ss. 24, 25, 48 or 49 of the 1993 Act (where there is a dispute)*.

6.4 Notices

6.4.1 Notice of claim to exercise right of collective enfranchisement or right to a new lease

The extended period over which negotiations will often take place under the 1993 Act makes it very desirable that the rights of the parties are protected in the register. The general rule is that registration by the tenants or tenant will be against the title of the freeholder or, in the case of a tenant claiming a new lease, against the competent landlord, who may or may not be the freeholder. However, it may also be desirable to register against other persons as well and this section considers when this might be done.

Any right of a tenant arising from a notice given under s. 13 of the 1993 Act (notice by qualifying tenants of flats of claim to exercise the right of collective enfranchisement) or s. 42 of the 1993 Act (notice by qualifying tenant of a flat of claim to exercise the right to a new lease) ("the 1993 Act notice") is not an interest with overriding status within the meaning of the LRA 2002 but may be

---

[152] See s. 58A of the 1993 Act, inserted by the Housing Act 1996.

protected on the register by a notice as if it were an estate contract (s. 97(1) of the 1993 Act).

If an application is made to enter an agreed notice under r.81 of the LRR 2003, the evidence in support should normally consist of a certified copy of the notice (which will be filed).

The entry in the charges register will be as follows:

> *"Notice entered pursuant to section 97(1) of the Leasehold Reform, Housing and Urban Development Act 1993 that a notice dated _____ has been served under section 13 [or 42] of that Act by _____ of _____. NOTE: Copy filed."* (There is no CRE for this entry.)

If the application is for a unilateral notice the statutory declaration or certificate will need to state that a notice was served by or on behalf of the beneficiary on the registered proprietor (who should be named) in accordance with ss. 13 or 42 of the 1993 Act on a stated date.

6.4.2 Vesting orders made under ss. 26(1) or 50(1) of the 1993 Act (where the relevant landlord cannot be found or identified)

The LRA 2002 applies to such an order as it applies to an order affecting land that is made by the Court for the purpose of enforcing a judgment (s. 97(2)(a) of the 1993 Act). You can, therefore, apply for such an order or application to the court for such an order to be protected by notice. A person who has applied for such an order who applies for a restriction in form N to Schedule 4 to the LRR 2003 and a person who has obtained an order who applies for a restriction in form L or N is regarded as having sufficient interest to apply for the restriction (rr.93(q) and (o) of the LRR 2003 respectively).

6.4.3 Orders made under ss. 24, 25, 48 or 49, 1993 Act (where there is a dispute)

There are no express provisions in the 1993 Act relating to the protection of such an order or an application to the court for such an order. However, in view of its nature, such an order or application to the court for such an order can be protected by a notice.

6.4.4 Protection against persons other than the freeholder or competent landlord

Collective enfranchisement

The 1993 Act provides that, after any initial notice has been served and registered, the freeholder cannot "make any disposal severing his interest in the premises or in any property specified in the notice" nor may he grant, in effect, any lease. Similarly, any intermediate lessee cannot grant any lease, although the leasehold interest itself can be sold or mortgaged (s. 19(1) of the 1993 Act). Any such grant or disposal is void.

Where the registrar is uncertain whether or not a disposition is caught by these provisions, he will require a certificate to be given by the solicitors to the freeholder that the transaction is not one to which the 1993 Act applies. This includes any disposition by a mortgagee under any power of sale. For these reasons, the registrar considers that the nominee purchaser should apply against all titles affected by the notice, not just that of the reversioner. Where any interest is not registered, a land charge should be registered.

Individual new flat leases
A tenant's notice severely restricts the right of the landlord and competent landlord to terminate the tenant's lease (Schedule 12 to the 1993 Act). Since it would seem undesirable for a purchaser from an intermediate lessee to be unaware of the position of the tenant, such a tenant should consider protecting the notice on any intermediate landlord's title, or at the Land Charges Department.

Generally
The 1993 Act makes considerable provision for the service of notices or counter notices. Most of these would not seem to be pending land actions. However, where there are specific applications to the court or to a tribunal, it would seem that they very well may be, for example an application to the court to defeat a tenant's claim on the grounds of redevelopment under s. 47(1), 1993 Act. In those cases, reversioners, intermediate landlords and tenants should consider carefully against whom the registration should be made.

6.4.5 Cancellation generally
Application for cancellation should be made in either form CN1 or UN4 and an application to remove a unilateral notice should be made in form UN2. In accordance with normal Land Registry practice, there will be no automatic cancellation of notices where an application is received to register a transfer of the freehold or new lease. Where the notice under the 1993 Act was protected by a caution, a withdrawal in form WCT should be lodged.

6.4.6 Later application to register a disposition where a notice made under s. 13 of the 1993 Act is protected in the register
Any application to register a disposition must include a certificate that the disposition is not one involving a disposal or grant of a lease within s. 19(1) of the 1993 Act. (This requirement also applies to a transfer by a mortgagee in exercise of their power of sale.) It does not matter whether the disposition is dated before or after the notice in the register.

Once you have supplied this certificate, we will then serve notice of your application on the beneficiary of the unilateral notice or the applicant for the agreed notice. If we receive no objection to the notice, we will complete the registration, but will **not** cancel the entry of the section 13 notice on the register.

6.4.7 Later application for agreed or unilateral notice where a notice made under s. 13 of the 1993 Act is protected in the register
We will generally ignore a section 13 notice where the later application is one to enter a unilateral or agreed notice. The exception to this general rule is where we

have had to satisfy ourselves as to the validity of the applicant's claim under s. 34(3)(c) of the 1993 Act. In that case, where it appears that the application may be to register a notice protecting an interest arising under a disposition falling with s. 19(1) of the 1993 Act, we will require a certificate and serve notice as referred to in section *6.4.6 Later application to register a disposition where a notice made under s. 13 of the 1993 Act is protected in the register.*

7 Flats: rights of tenants of flats under the Landlord and Tenant Act 1987

7.1 Generally
The 1987 Act gives certain rights to tenants of flats as against their landlord that continue to exist alongside the more general provisions of the 1993 Act. In certain cases, as mentioned in section *7.2 Notices*, the rights may require an entry to be made in the register if the title to the lease or to the reversion is registered. As mentioned in section *7.4 Variation of leases* the terms of the lease may also be varied.

7.2 Notices

7.2.1 Tenant's right of first refusal to purchase the reversion
A landlord of a building containing flats must not dispose or contract to dispose of an interest in those premises unless he has served a notice of his intention on the tenants giving them collectively a right of first refusal (ss. 1(1), 4A and 5(1) of the 1987 Act).

There are detailed definitions of what is meant by the landlord, a disposal, the premises and a qualifying tenant, and there are prescribed procedures that must be followed from the serving of the initial notice to the stage where the landlord disposes of his interest to the tenants or becomes free to dispose of it elsewhere.

It is also clearly stated in connection with these procedures that any reference to an offer is a reference to an offer made subject to contract, and any reference to the acceptance of an offer is a reference to its acceptance subject to contract (s. 20(2) of the 1987 Act). There is, in those circumstances, no interest capable of being protected on the register. However, once a contract has been entered into, the tenants can protect their interest by applying for the entry of a notice on the landlord's title or an entry at the Land Charges Department in the usual way.

Where a landlord has disposed of an interest in the premises in contravention of the tenants' right of first refusal, the tenants have additional rights, including, where applicable, the right to take the benefit of the contract, the right to compel the purchaser to sell to them or, in the case of a surrender, the right to a new lease.[152A] The notice by which the right is exercised does not itself give an interest that can be protected on the register but when a binding contract has been entered into in pursuance of a purchase notice, the tenants' interest may be protected by a notice in the usual way.

[152A] ss. 11, 11A, 12A–D, 13–14, 16–17 of, and Part I of Sch. 1 to, the 1987 Act.

7.2.2 Appointment of managers (of the block of flats)

A tenant of a building containing flats may apply to the court for the appointment of a manager if the landlord has failed to manage the premises in accordance with his obligations or the service charges are unreasonable (s. 21 of the 1987 Act). The court may then, if it thinks fit, make an order appointing a manager to carry out functions in connection with management or functions of a receiver. Any such order will be registrable as an order appointing a receiver or sequestrator of land.[152B] In the case of registered land this requires protection by the registration of a restriction. This jurisdiction has been transferred to leasehold valuation tribunals.[152C]

7.2.3 Compulsory acquisition by tenants of their landlord's interest

Where a landlord of a building containing flats is in breach of his obligations to its tenants in regard to the maintenance or management of the premises, the court may, on the application of the tenants, make an acquisition order (ss. 25, 28 and 29 of the 1987 Act). If it decides to make an order, the court will provide for a person nominated by the tenants to be entitled to acquire the landlord's interest in the premises on such terms as may be agreed, or, failing agreement, on such terms as a leasehold valuation tribunal may determine (ss. 30 and 31 of the 1987 Act).

An application for an acquisition order is registrable as a pending land action so that, in the case of registered land, it may be protected by a notice. When an acquisition order has been made, it will be registrable as an order affecting land made by the court for the purpose of enforcing a judgment and, in the case of registered land, it may also be protected by the entry of a notice. A person who has applied for an acquisition order under s. 28 of the 1987 Act who applies for a restriction in form N to Schedule 4 to the LRR 2003 and a person who has similarly obtained an acquisition order and applies for a restriction in form L or N is regarded as having sufficient interest to apply for the restriction (rr.93(o) and (n) of the LRR 2003 respectively).

7.3 Registration following an acquisition order

This section deals with applications for first registration of unregistered land following an acquisition order made under the 1987 Act, and applications for registration of the tenants' nominee where an acquisition order is made in respect of land that is already registered.

7.3.1 First registration

Make the application in the usual way on form FR1. Where there has been no transfer the application should be accompanied by:

—an office copy of the court order, duly stamped;

—confirmation of the payment into court;

[152B] s. 24(8) of the 1987 Act; s. 87(2)(a) of the LRA 2002.
[152C] s. 86, Housing Act 1996. As to leasehold valuation tribunals see s. 52A of the 1987 Act.

—any available evidence of the former landlord's title.

If no documentary evidence of the title is available, we suggest that you apply for a possessory title, supported by a statutory declaration by a person having the necessary knowledge of the facts—normally a director or the secretary or solicitor or licensed conveyancer of the applicant company. Since they may not be aware of disputes between the former landlord and third parties, they may only be able to speak as to the period for which the applicant has held the land.

7.3.2 Registration of nominee as proprietor
Make the application in the usual way in form AP1. Where there has been no transfer the application should be accompanied by an office copy of the court order, duly stamped, and confirmation of the payment into court. Notice of the application will be served on the registered proprietor and any other persons appearing from the register to be interested in the title. If no objection is received the registration will be completed, if necessary under a new title number.

7.4 Variation of leases
Any party to a long lease of a flat may apply to the court for an order varying the lease on the grounds that the lease fails to make satisfactory provision with respect to repair, maintenance, the provision of services, insurance, the recovery of expenses or the computation of service charges (s. 35 of the 1987 Act). The court may then make an appropriate order that will be binding on the parties to the lease and any other persons concerned (ss. 38 and 39 of the 1987 Act). The entry of the variation order on the register of the titles affected will be dealt with in the same way as a deed of variation.

8 Enquiries and comments

If you have a particular concern that is not covered by this guide, please contact Land Registry in advance of the transaction—see the *Contact details* panel on the front cover of this guide. If the transaction is particularly complex, it may be better to make your enquiry in writing at the Land Registry office that will process your application.

If you have any comments or suggestions about our guides, please send them to:

Registration Change Group
Land Registry
Lincoln's Inn Fields
London WC2A 3PH
(DX 1098 London/Chancery Lane WC2)

You can obtain further copies of this and all our guides free of charge from any Land Registry office or you can download them from our website in English or Welsh.

Appendix 1—Merger of leases on acquisition of the freehold

When a person is entitled, in the same capacity, to the leasehold and any superior leasehold and the freehold titles to a property, the leasehold titles will be merged if the registered proprietor or their practitioner makes an application for merger and any entries on the inferior title(s) that would prevent merger are cancelled or removed.

The mechanics of the application depend on the circumstances of the case, as explained below. If you cannot produce the lease for any reason (for example where the lease is not in the lessee's possession because it affects also other land) a short letter stating the reason for its non-production should be lodged.

Merger of registered leases

When the freehold title is already registered, the request for closure of the leasehold title(s) may be made in panel 5 of form AP1, which should refer to the title numbers of the titles to be closed.

When the freehold title is the subject of an application for first registration, the request for merger should be made in panel 4 of form FR1 and in addition form AP1 should be lodged for closure of the leasehold title(s). The lease should accompany the application. The registered leasehold title can only be closed when all entries on the register have been satisfactorily dealt with.

Any restriction on the register must normally be withdrawn by means of a form RX3 signed by the restrictioner or his/her conveyancer, unless a corresponding restriction is to be entered against the freehold title.

A restriction in favour of a chargee will be cancelled automatically when the title is closed (and re-entered on the new title if the charge is to be registered against it).

A form A restriction on dispositions by a sole proprietor will also be cancelled automatically on closure of the title.

An inhibition resulting from an injunction or restraint order may prevent the closure of the title, or a restriction may be entered on the freehold title, depending on the terms of the court order on which the entry is founded. It may be cancelled on production of an official copy of the court order that puts an end to the original order.

Application should be made for the cancellation or removal of any notice on forms CN1, UN4 or UN2 as appropriate.

Evidence to support certain applications is listed below.

When a registered charge appears on the title a discharge of the charge, or a deed of substituted security, must be produced.

Where a noted charge appears on the title it must be produced with a receipt endorsed or other evidence of discharge, or a deed of substituted security.

A creditor's notice on the leasehold title will normally be entered on the freehold title. If no longer required, the notice may be cancelled on application accompanied by an office copy of the court order dismissing or withdrawing the petition in bankruptcy or rescinding or annulling the subsequent bankruptcy order.

A bankruptcy inhibition registered under the Land Registration Act 1925, or a restriction registered under s. 86 of the LRA 2002, may be cancelled on production of an official copy of the court order under which the bankruptcy order was rescinded or annulled.

An inhibition resulting from an injunction or restraint order may prevent the closure of the title, or a restriction may be entered on the freehold title, depending on the terms of the court order on which the entry is founded. It may be cancelled on production of an official copy of the court order that puts an end to the original order.

A (matrimonial) homes rights notice that no longer affects the title may be withdrawn by means of an application in form HR4. If not withdrawn or cancelled, the notice will be carried forward onto the freehold title.

A notice of an access order under the Access to Neighbouring Land Act 1992 may be cancelled on production of the appropriate evidence, and if not cancelled will likewise be carried forward onto the freehold title.

A caution may be withdrawn by means of form WCT.

Merger of unregistered lease noted against a registered superior title
Make the application in form CN1, supported by the lease and all deeds and documents relating to the leasehold title. The documents lodged should include an up-to-date land charges search.

Merger of unregistered lease not noted against a registered superior title
If the superior title is being registered or is the subject of an application in form CN1, the lease should be referred to in the application.

If the superior title is already registered and the lease is not noted against it, no application for merger is required. In either case the original lease and all deeds and documents relating to the title to it should be lodged. The documents lodged should include an up-to-date land charges search.

Appendix 2—Applications for registration of extended leases

Registration of new lease
The application for registration of the new lease should be made in form FR1 if the reversionary title is unregistered, or form AP1 if the reversionary title is registered.

The application should be accompanied by:

— the lease being registered, duly stamped (ad valorem on the amount of the premium and the rent reserved, if any, and "Produced" stamp under s. 28 of the Finance Act 1931), together with a certified copy;

— evidence of the lessor's title to grant the lease, if required;

— consent of lessor's mortgagee, if required;

— any consent required by a restriction affecting the lessor's title;

—particulars of any leases intermediate between the lessor's title and the new lease (see section *6.3.4 Reversionary titles, Intermediate leasehold titles*);

—application to give effect to the deemed surrender of the existing lease and any intermediate lease held by or in trust for the applicant;

—application for any necessary restriction or notice on the title to the new lease;

—fees.

The new lease may either be a complete, full length lease, or it may be drawn by reference to the terms of the lease being surrendered. Avoid using a deed of variation. The effect of the procedure may appear to be the variation of the length of the term of the original lease but this is not the case. The new lease takes effect in substitution for the existing lease.

Lessor's title

If the lessor's title is unregistered, an examined abstract or epitome of the lessor's title, and a current search in Land Charges Department, should be obtained and lodged with the application, with a view to the grant of an absolute leasehold title. Normally an absolute leasehold title can be granted only if the lessor's title and any superior titles have previously been approved by Land Registry on an application for first registration or are lodged with the application.

Consent of lessor's mortgagee

The consent of the lessor's mortgagee (and any other person interested in the mortgage) should be lodged where the old lease:

—was granted on or after 1 November 1993 (for applications under the 1993 Act) or 1 January 1968 (for applications under the 1967 Act);

—was made subsequent to the date of the lessor's mortgage; and

—would not have been binding on the persons interested in the mortgage (ie it was outside the mortgagor's leasing powers and they did not concur in it).

Where, however, the consent is not lodged, the following entry will be made in the property register of the new title:

"The title to the lease is, during the subsistence of the charge dated . . . . in favour of . . . . affecting the lessor's title (and to the extent permitted by law, any charge replacing or varying this charge or any further charge in respect of all or part of the sum secured by this charge), subject to any rights that may have arisen by reason of the absence of chargee's consent, unless the lease is authorised by section 99 of the Law of Property Act 1925."

This entry will not be made if a copy of the mortgage deed is lodged together with confirmation that the granting of the lease was permitted by the terms of the mortgage (by referring to the relevant clause in the deed) and that the mortgagee's consent was not required.

NB: A consent is always required where there is a restriction in favour of the lessor's mortgagee on the lessor's title.

In other cases the power of the lessor to grant the lease cannot be questioned on account of the existence of a mortgage on its title.

Application to give effect to the deemed surrender of the existing lease

The form of this application will depend on whether the existing lease is registered, whether the surrendered lease is noted on any reversionary title, and whether the application is under the 1967 Act or the 1993 Act.

If the applicant's existing leasehold title is registered, application should be made to give effect to the surrender of the existing lease by closing that title. If the applicant's leasehold title is not registered but notice of it is entered on any reversionary title, you must make an application for the cancellation of the notice.

Even if the surrendered lease is neither registered nor noted on any reversionary title, it is still necessary for the surrendered lease and the applicant's title to it to be lodged, together with a current Land Charges Department search. Any mortgages affecting the lease should also be lodged. Any mortgagees of the applicant's existing lease should be contacted prior to completion of the new lease and the necessary arrangements made.

Any other interest affecting the existing lease should also be carefully considered. If it is protected in the register of the existing lease but does not affect the new lease, lodge an application for the withdrawal of the restriction, or notice of deposit or intended deposit, or the cancellation of the notice. If it, or a corresponding interest, affects the new lease, an application to protect it by means of a suitable entry in the register should be included in, or accompany, the application to register the new lease.

Closure of existing leasehold title

Make the application to close the applicant's existing title on form AP1 and describe the application in panel 5 as 'Closure of leasehold title'. The original lease should accompany the application.

Cancellation of notice of existing lease on reversionary title (when existing lease is unregistered)

Make the application in form CN1. The surrendered lease and the applicant's title to it should be lodged, together with a current Land Charges Department search. Any mortgages affecting the lease should also be lodged.

Arrangements with mortgagees

Where the new lease is being granted under the 1993 Act, any charges on the surrendered lease will transfer automatically. The applicant should apply for registration of the charge in panels 5 and 13 of form AP1 or panels 4 and 10 of form FR1, the form used depending on whether the reversioner's title is registered. It is only necessary to arrange for the charge to be lodged if the surrendered lease is unregistered. If the charge is to be protected by notice only, and the reversioner's title is registered, you should complete either form AN1 or UN1, as appropriate.

Where, however, the new lease is being granted under the 1967 Act, a mortgage does not transfer automatically to the new lease and should, therefore, either be discharged and replaced, or transferred to the new lease by deed. If the mortgage is discharged, the discharged mortgage and evidence of discharge and the new mortgage, if any, with a certified copy if the new mortgage is to be registered, should be lodged with the application. If a deed of substituted security is used, the mortgage should be lodged together with the deed and, if the mortgage is to be registered against the new title, a certified copy.

If the mortgagee's cooperation cannot be secured, Land Registry will endeavour to serve a special notice on them, and any other person appearing to be interested in the mortgage, giving details of:

—the mortgage;

—the applicants and the nature of the application;

—the intended closure of the title to the existing lease (if registered);

—the intended cancellation of the notice of the existing lease on a superior title (if the existing lease is not registered but is noted on such a title);

—the effect of the application, if completed, on the mortgage;

—how any objection to the application can be made; and requesting the lodging of the original mortgage.

If there is no response to the notice, the application will be completed. In the case of a lease granted under the 1993 Act, the mortgage may be registered or noted against the new title in the normal way. In the case of a lease granted under the 1967 Act, a special entry will be made, as described in section *5.4.2 Entries in the register*.

If, in response to the notice, the recipient lodges the original mortgage, it will either be registered or noted. If notice has to be served in respect of more than one subsisting mortgage, separate entries will be made in the register according to the respective priorities of the mortgages concerned.

Other entries on existing leasehold title
A restriction in favour of a chargee will be cancelled automatically when the old title is closed (and re-entered on the new title if the charge is registered against it). A form A restriction against dispositions by a sole proprietor will also be cancelled on closure of the title. A voluntary restriction in the register of the old title must normally be withdrawn by means of a form RX3 signed by the restrictioner or their conveyancer, unless a corresponding restriction is applied for against the new lease.

Application should be made for the cancellation or removal of any notices other than one protecting a monetary charge, on forms CN1, UN4 or UN2 as appropriate.

Evidence to support certain applications is set out below. A creditor's notice will normally be entered on the new title. If no longer required, application should be accompanied by an office copy of the court order dismissing or withdrawing the petition in bankruptcy or rescinding or annulling the subsequent bankruptcy order. A bankruptcy restriction may be cancelled on production of an official copy of the court order under which the bankruptcy order was rescinded or annulled.

A homes rights notice that no longer affects may be withdrawn by means of an application in form HR4. If not withdrawn or cancelled, the notice will be carried forward onto the new title.

A notice of an access order under the Access to Neighbouring Land Act 1992 requires production of the appropriate evidence, and if not cancelled will be carried forward onto the new title.

A caution may be withdrawn by means of a form WCT.

An inhibition resulting from an injunction or restraint order may prevent the closure of the title or a restriction may be entered on the freehold title, depending on the terms of the court order on which the entry is founded. It may be cancelled on production of an official copy of the court order that puts an end to the original order.

We will consider any entry affecting the old title that is not withdrawn or cancelled and is not carried forward onto, or replaced by a corresponding entry on, the new title on a case-by-case basis. In some cases it may be possible to deal with the matter by the service of notice.

Protection of interests affecting the new lease

As with all applications for registration of a lease, full particulars of all third party interests affecting the lease must be entered in the appropriate panel of the application form AP1/FR1 and separate applications made for their entry on the register where appropriate. In addition to this, any restriction required must be applied for in form RX1.

Add the following appendices:

APPENDIX 2S

Commonhold and Leasehold Reform Act 2002 (Commencement No.2 and Savings) (Wales) Order 2004

(SI 2004/669 (W.62))

The National Assembly for Wales, in exercise of the powers conferred upon it by **1218S** section 181 of the Commonhold and Leasehold Reform Act 2002,[153] hereby makes the following Order:

Citation, interpretation and application

1.—(1) This Order may be cited as the Commonhold and Leasehold Reform Act 2002 (Commencement No.2 and Savings) (Wales) Order 2004.

(2) In this Order—

> "LVT" ("*TPL*") means a leasehold valuation tribunal;
>
> "the 1967 Act" ("*Deddf 1967*") means the Leasehold Reform Act 1967;[154]
>
> "the 1985 Act" ("*Deddf 1985*") means the Landlord and Tenant Act 198;[155]
>
> "the 1987 Act" ("*Deddf 1987*") means the Landlord and Tenant Act 1987;[156]
>
> "the 1993 Act" ("*Deddf 1993*") means the Leasehold Reform, Housing and Urban Development Act 1993;[157]
>
> "the 1996 Act" ("*Deddf 1996*") means the Housing Act 1996;[158]
>
> References to sections and Schedules are, unless otherwise stated, references to sections of, and Schedules to, the Commonhold and Leasehold Reform Act 2002; and
>
> any reference to a repeal is to a repeal made by section 180 and Schedule 14.

(3) This Order applies to Wales only.

Provisions coming into force on 30th March 2004

2.—The following provisions will come into force on 30th March 2004—

> (a) sections 71 to 73, 75 to 77, 79, 81 to 83 , 85 to 91, 93 to 103, 105 to 109, 111 to 113, 159, 163, 173, Schedules 6 and 7;
>
> (b) sections 74, 78, 80, 84, 92, 110, 174 and Schedule 12 to the extent that they are not already in force; and
>
> (c) subject to the savings in Schedule 2 to this Order—

    (i) sections 148, 149, 150, 155, 157 in so far as it relates to paragraphs 8 to 13 of Schedule 10, 158, 175, 176 in so far as it relates to paragraphs 1 to 15 of Schedule 13, Schedule 9, paragraphs 8 to 13 of Schedule 10, Schedule 11 and paragraphs 1 to 15 of Schedule 13;

    (ii) subsections (1) to (5) of section 172 except in so far as they relate to the application to the Crown of sections 152 to 154, 164 to 171, paragraphs 1 to 7 of Schedule 10 and paragraph 16 of Schedule 13;

    (iii) subsection (6) of section 172 except in so far as the substitutions made by that subsection relate to sections 42A and 42B of the 1987 Act;

    (iv) to the extent that it is not already in force, section 180 in so far as it relates to the repeals in Schedule 14 which are set out in Schedule 1 to this Order;

[. . .]

Signed on behalf of the National Assembly for Wales under section 66(1) of the Government of Wales Act 1998.[159]

John Marek
The Deputy Presiding Officer of the National Assembly
9th March 2004

Article 2(c)(iv)   Schedule 1

REPEALS

PART 1

LEASEHOLD VALUATION TRIBUNALS

Short Title and Chapter	Extent of Repeal
Leasehold Reform Act 1967 (c. 88)	Section 21(1A) and (3) to (4A).
Housing Act 1980 (c. 51)	In section 142— Subsection (2) and in subsection (3), the words from the beginning to "and". In Schedule 22— Part 1, and in Part 2, paragraph 8(4) to (6).
Landlord and Tenant Act 1985 (c. 70)	Sections 31A to 31C. In the Schedule, paragraph 8(5).

Short Title and Chapter	Extent of Repeal
Landlord and Tenant Act 1987 (c.31)	Section 23(2). Sections 24A and 24B. In section 38, in the sidenote, the words "by the court". Section 52A. In section 53(2); the words "under section 52A(3) or".
Tribunals and Inquiries Act 1992 (c.53)	In Schedule 3, paragraph 13.
Leasehold Reform, Housing and Urban Development Act 1993 (c.28)	Section 75(4) and (5). In section 88— in subsection (2)(b), the words "constituted for the purposes of that Part of that Act", and subsections (3) to (5) and (7).
Leasehold Reform, Housing and Urban Development Act 1993	In section 91— in subsection (1), the words from the beginning to "this section; and", subsections (3) to (8), subsection (10), and in subsection (11), the words from "and the reference" to the end. In section 94, in subsection (10), the words from "and references in this subsection" to the end. In section 101(1), the definition of "rent assessment committee".
Housing Act 1996 (c.52)	Section 83(3). Section 86(4) and (5). Section 119. In Schedule 6, in Part 4, paragraphs 7 and 8.

Article 2(c)   Schedule 2

SAVINGS

Absent landlords—leasehold houses

1.—The amendments made by sections 148 and 149 will not have effect in relation to an application for enfranchisement made under section 27 of the 1967 Act before 31st March 2004.

[. . .]

Charges under estate management schemes

10.—Section 159 will not apply to a charge under an estate management scheme that was payable before 31st March 2004.

[. . .]

186   APPENDIX 2S

Leasehold valuation tribunals

13.—Section 175, the amendments made by section 176 and Schedule 13 and the repeals in Part 1 of Schedule 1 to this Order will not have effect in relation to—

(a) any application made to a LVT; or
(b) any proceedings transferred to a LVT by a county court,

before 31st March 2004.

Add new Footnote 153: 2002 c.15.
Add new Footnote 154: 1967 c.88.
Add new Footnote 155: 1985 c.70.
Add new Footnote 156: 1987 c.31.
Add new Footnote 157: 1993 c.28.
Add new Footnote 158: 1996 c.52.
Add new Footnote 159: 1998 c.38.

APPENDIX 2T

Leasehold Reform (Collective Enfranchisement and Lease Renewal) (Amendment) (Wales) Regulations 2004

(SI 2004/670 (W.63))

The National Assembly for Wales, in exercise of the powers conferred on the Secretary of State by section 98 of the Leasehold Reform, Housing and Urban Development Act 1993[160] and now vested in the National Assembly for Wales,[161] hereby makes the following Regulations: **1218T**

Name and commencement

1.—These Regulations are called the Leasehold Reform (Collective Enfranchisement and Lease Renewal) (Amendment) (Wales) Regulations 2004 and shall come into force on the 31st March 2004.

Application

2.—These Regulations apply only—

(a) in respect of premises in Wales;

(b) to cases where a notice under section 13 (notice by qualifying tenants of claim to exercise right to collectively enfranchise) or section 42 (notice by qualifying tenant of claim to exercise right to acquire a new lease) of the Leasehold Reform, Housing and Urban Development Act 1993 is served on or after the date these Regulations come into force.

Amendments

3.—The Leasehold Reform (Collective Enfranchisement and Lease Renewal) Regulations 1993[162] shall be amended as follows—

(a) delete paragraph 2 of Schedule 1; and

(b) for sub-paragraph 4(1) of Schedule 2 substitute—

> "(1) The landlord may require the tenant to deduce his title to his tenancy, by giving him notice within the period of twenty one days beginning with the relevant date.".

Signed on behalf of the National Assembly for Wales under section 66(1) of the Government of Wales Act 1998.[163]

John Marek
The Deputy Presiding Officer of the National Assembly
9th March 2004

Add new Footnote 160: 1993 c.28.

Add new Footnote 161: The powers of the Secretary of State under s. 98 of the Leasehold Reform, Housing and Urban Development Act 1993 were transferred to the National Assembly for Wales pursuant to art. 2(2) of, and Sch. 1 to, the National Assembly for Wales (Transfer of Functions) Order 1999 (SI 1999/672).

Add new Footnote 162: SI 1993/2407.

Add new Footnote 163: 1998 c.38.

APPENDIX 2U

Leasehold Valuation Tribunals (Procedure) (Wales) Regulations 2004

(SI 2004/681 (W.69))

The National Assembly for Wales, in exercise of the powers vested in it under **1218U**
section 35(5) of the Landlord and Tenant Act 1987[164] and Schedule 12 to the
Commonhold and Leasehold Reform Act 2002,[165] and after consultation with the
Council on Tribunals, hereby makes the following Regulations:

Name, commencement, and application
 1.—(1) These Regulations are called the Leasehold Valuation Tribunals (Procedure) (Wales) Regulations 2004.
 (2) These Regulations shall come into force on 31st March 2004.
 (3) These Regulations apply in relation to any application made, or proceedings transferred from a court, to a leasehold valuation tribunal[166] in respect of
premises in Wales on or after 31st March 2004.

Interpretation
 2.—In these Regulations—

   "the 1985 Act" ("*Deddf 1985*") means the Landlord and Tenant Act
     1985;[167]
   "the 1987 Act" ("*Deddf 1987*") means the Landlord and Tenant Act
     1987;
   "the 1993 Act" ("*Deddf 1993*") means the Leasehold Reform, Housing and
     Urban Development Act 1993;[168]
   "the 2002 Act" ("*Deddf 2002*") means the Commonhold and Leasehold
     Reform Act 2002;
   "applicant" ("*ceisydd*") means—

     (a) the person making an application to a tribunal, or
     (b) the person who is the claimant or applicant in proceedings before a
         court which are transferred by order of the court to a tribunal;

   "application" ("*cais*") means, other than for the purposes of regulations 1,
     20 and 25—

     (a) an application to a tribunal of a description specified in Schedule 1,
         or
     (b) a transferred application;

   "recognised tenants' association" ("*cymdeithas tenantiaid cydnabydde-
     dig*") has the same meaning as in section 29 of the 1985 Act;[169]
   "representative application" ("*cais cynrychioladol*") has the meaning given
     in regulation 8;

"respondent" ("*atebydd*") means—

    (a) the person against whom an applicant seeks an order or determination from a tribunal; or

    (b) the person who is the defendant or respondent in proceedings before a court which are transferred by order of the court to a tribunal;

"transferred application" ("*cais a drosglwyddwyd*") means so much of proceedings before a court as relate to a question falling within the jurisdiction of a tribunal as have been transferred to the tribunal for determination by order of the court; and

"tribunal" ("*tribiwnlys*") means a leasehold valuation tribunal.

Particulars of applications

3.—(1) The particulars to be included with an application are—

    (a) the name and address of the applicant;

    (b) the name and address of the respondent;

    (c) the name and address of any landlord or tenant of the premises to which the application relates;

    (d) the address of the premises to which the application relates; and

    (e) a statement that the applicant believes that the facts stated in the application are true.

(2) Where an application is of a description specified in paragraph 1 of Schedule 1 (enfranchisement and extended leases) the particulars and documents listed in paragraph 1 of Schedule 2 shall be included with the application.

(3) Where an application is of a description specified in paragraph 2 of Schedule 1 (service charges, administration charges and estate charges) the particulars and documents listed in paragraph 2 of Schedule 2 shall be included with the application.

(4) Where an application is of a description specified in paragraph 3 of Schedule 1 (estate management schemes) the particulars and documents listed in paragraph 3 of Schedule 2 shall be included with the application.

(5) Where an application is of a description specified in paragraph 4 of Schedule 1 (right to manage) the particulars and documents listed in paragraph 4 of Schedule 2 shall be included with the application.

(6) Where an application is of a description specified in paragraph 5 of Schedule 1 (appointment of manager) the particulars and documents listed in paragraph 5 of Schedule 2 shall be included with the application.

(7) Where an application is of a description specified in paragraph 6 of Schedule 1 (variation of leases) the particulars and documents listed in paragraph 6 of Schedule 2 shall be included with the application.

(8) Any of the requirements in the preceding paragraphs may be dispensed with or relaxed if the tribunal is satisfied that—

    (a) the particulars and documents included with an application are sufficient to enable the application to be determined; and

(b) no prejudice will, or is likely to, be caused to any party to the application.

Notice of application by tribunal

5.—(1) On receipt of an application, other than an application made under Part 4 of the 1987 Act, the tribunal shall send a copy of the application and each of the documents accompanying it to each person named in it as a respondent.

(2) On receipt of an application of a description specified in paragraph 2 of Schedule 1 (service charges, administration charges and estate charges), the tribunal shall give notice of the application to—

(a) the secretary of any recognised tenants' association mentioned in the particulars included in the application; and

(b) any person, whose name and address the tribunal has, who the tribunal considers is likely to be significantly affected by the application.

(3) On receipt of an application the tribunal may give notice to any other person it considers appropriate.

(4) Any notice given under paragraph (2) or (3) shall include a statement that any person may make a request to the tribunal under regulation 6 to be joined as a party to the proceedings with details as to how such a request can be made.

(5) Any notice given under paragraph (2) or (3) may be given by local advertisement.

(6) In this regulation, "local advertisement" means publication of the notice in two newspapers (at least one of which should be a freely distributed newspaper) circulating in the locality in which the premises to which the application relates is situated.

Request to be treated as an applicant or respondent

6.—(1) Any person may make a request to the tribunal to be joined as a party to the proceedings.

(2) Any request under paragraph (1)—

(a) may be made without notice; and

(b) shall specify whether the person making the request wishes to be treated as—

(i) an applicant; or

(ii) a respondent,

to the application.

(3) The tribunal may grant or refuse a request under paragraph (1).

(4) As soon as possible after reaching its decision on a request under paragraph (1), the tribunal shall—

(a) notify the person making the request of the decision and the reasons for it; and

(b) send a copy of the notification to the applicant and the respondent.

(5) Any person whose request under paragraph (1) is granted shall be treated as an applicant or respondent, as the case may be, for the purposes of regulations 8 to 18, 20 and 24.

(6) In the regulations mentioned in paragraph (5) any reference to—

(a) an applicant, or
(b) a respondent,

shall be construed as including a person treated as such under this regulation and any reference to a party shall be construed as including any such person.

Non-payment of fees

7.—(1) In any case where a fee which is payable under regulation 4 or 5 of the Leasehold Valuation Tribunals (Fees) (Wales) Regulations 2004[170] is not paid in accordance with those Regulations, the tribunal shall not proceed further with the application to which the fee relates until the fee is paid.

(2) Where a fee remains unpaid for a period of one month from the date on which it becomes due, the application shall be treated as withdrawn unless the tribunal is satisfied that there are reasonable grounds not to do so.

Representative applications and other provisions for securing consistency

8.—(1) Where it appears to a tribunal that numerous applications—

(a) have been made in respect of the same or substantially the same matters; or
(b) include some matters which are the same or substantially the same,

the tribunal may propose to determine only one of those applications ("the representative application") as representative of all of the applications on those matters which are the same or substantially the same ("the common matters"), and shall give notice of the proposal to the parties to all such applications.

(2) A notice under paragraph (1) shall—

(a) specify the common matters;
(b) specify the application which the tribunal proposes to determine as the representative application;
(c) explain that the tribunal's decision on the common matters in the representative application will apply to the common matters in any application made by a person to whom notice has been given under that paragraph;
(d) invite objections to the tribunal's proposal to determine the representative application; and
(e) specify the address to which objections may be sent and the date (being not less than 21 days after the date that the notice was sent) by which the objections must be received by the tribunal.

(3) Where no objection is received on or before the date specified in the notice—

(a) the tribunal shall determine the representative application in accordance with these Regulations;

(b) the tribunal need not determine the matters mentioned in paragraph (1)(a) in any other application made by a person to whom a notice under paragraph (1) has been given; and

(c) the decision of the tribunal in respect of the representative application shall be recorded as the decision of the tribunal in respect of the common matters in any such other application.

(4) Where an objection is received on or before the date specified in the notice—

(a) sub-paragraphs (a) to (c) of paragraph (3) shall apply only to those applications in respect of which no objection was made; and

(b) the application in respect of which an objection was made may be determined together with the representative application.

Subsequent applications where notice of the representative application given

9.—(1) If, after a representative application has been determined, a subsequent application is made which includes any of the common matters on which the tribunal has made a decision in its determination of the representative application, and the applicant is a person to whom a notice under regulation 8(1) was given, the tribunal shall give notice to the parties to the subsequent application of—

(a) the matters which, in the opinion of the tribunal, are the common matters in the subsequent application and the representative application;

(b) the decision recorded in respect of the common matters in the representative application;

(c) the date on which notice under regulation 8(1) was given to the applicant;

(d) the tribunal's proposal to record the tribunal's decision on the common matters in the subsequent application in identical terms to the decision in the representative application;

(e) the address to which objections to the tribunal's proposal may be sent and the date (being not less than 21 days after the date that the notice was sent) by which such objections must be received by the tribunal; and

(f) a statement that any objection must include the grounds on which it is made and, in particular, whether it is alleged that the notice under regulation 8(1) was not received by the person making the objection.

(2) Where no objection is received on or before the date specified in the notice—

(a) the tribunal need not determine the matters mentioned in paragraph
    1(a); and
(b) the decision of the tribunal in respect of the common matters in the
    representative application shall be recorded as the decision of the
    tribunal in respect of the common matters in the subsequent applica-
    tion.

(3) Where an objection is received to the tribunal's proposal on or before the
date specified in the notice—

(a) the tribunal shall consider the objection when determining the sub-
    sequent application; and
(b) if the tribunal dismisses the objection, it may record the decision
    mentioned in paragraph (1)(b) as the decision of the tribunal in the
    subsequent application.

Subsequent applications where notice of representative application not given

10.—(1) If, after a representative application has been determined, a subsequent application is made which includes an of the common matters on which
the tribunal has made a decision in its determination of the representative
application, and the applicant is not a person to whom a notice under regulation
8(1) was given, the tribunal shall give notice to the parties to the subsequent
application of—

(a) the matters which, in the opinion of the tribunal, are the common
    matters in the subsequent application and the representative applica-
    tion;
(b) the decision recorded in respect of those common matters in the repre-
    sentative application;
(c) the tribunal's proposal to record its decision on the common matters in
    the subsequent application in identical terms to the decision in the
    representative application; and
(d) the address to which objections to the tribunal's proposal may be sent
    and the date (being not less than 21 days after the date that the notice
    was sent) by which such objections must be received by the tribunal.

(2) Where no objection is received on or before the date specified in the
notice—

(a) the tribunal need not determine the matters mentioned in paragraph
    (1)(a); and
(b) the decision of the tribunal in respect of the common matters in the
    representative application shall be recorded as the decision of the
    tribunal in respect of the common matters in the subsequent applica-
    tion.

(3) Where an objection is received to the tribunal's proposal on or before the date specified in the notice the tribunal shall determine the application in accordance with the following provisions of these Regulations.

Dismissal of frivolous etc. applications

11.—(1) Subject to paragraph (2), where—

(a) it appears to a tribunal that an application is frivolous or vexatious or otherwise an abuse of process of the tribunal; or

(b) the respondent to an application makes a request to the tribunal to dismiss an application as frivolous or vexatious or otherwise an abuse of the process of the tribunal,

the tribunal may dismiss the application, in whole or in part.

(2) Before dismissing an application under paragraph (1) the tribunal shall give notice to the applicant in accordance with paragraph (3).

(3) Any notice under paragraph (2) shall state—

(a) that the tribunal is minded to dismiss the application;

(b) the grounds on which it is minded to dismiss the application;

(c) the date (being not less than 21 days after the date that the notice was sent) before which the applicant may request to appear before and be heard by the tribunal on the question whether the application should be dismissed.

(4) An application may not be dismissed unless—

(a) the applicant makes no request to the tribunal before the date mentioned in paragraph (3)(c); or

(b) where the applicant makes such a request, the tribunal has heard the applicant and the respondent, or such of them as attend the hearing, on the question of the dismissal of the application.

Pre-trial review

12.—(1) The tribunal may, whether on its own initiative or at the request of a party, hold a pre-trial review in respect of an application.

(2) The tribunal shall give the parties not less than 14 days notice (or such shorter notice as the parties agree to) of the date, time and place of the pre-trial review.

(3) At the pre-trial review the tribunal shall—

(a) give any direction that appears to the tribunal necessary or desirable for securing the just, expeditious and economical disposal of proceedings;

(b) endeavour to secure that the parties make all such admissions and agreements as ought reasonably to be made by them in relation to the proceedings; and

(c) record in any order made at the pre-trial review any such admission or agreement or any refusal to make such admission or agreement.

(4) The functions of the tribunal in relation to, or at, a pre-trial review may be exercised by any single member of the panel provided for in Schedule 10 to the Rent Act 1977[171] who is qualified to exercise them.[172]

Determination without a hearing

13.—(1) A tribunal may determine an application without an oral hearing, in accordance with the following provisions of this regulation, if—

(a) the respondent states in writing that he does not oppose the application;
(b) the respondent withdraws any opposition to the application; or
(c) the applicant and respondent so agree in writing.

(2) The tribunal shall—

(a) notify the parties that the application is to be determined without an oral hearing;
(b) invite written representations on the application;
(c) set time limits for sending any written representations to the tribunal; and
(d) set out how the tribunal intends to determine the matter without an oral hearing.

(3) At any time before the application is determined—

(a) the applicant or the respondent may make a request to the tribunal to be heard; or
(b) the tribunal may give notice to the parties that it intends to determine the application at a hearing in accordance with regulation 14.

(4) Where a request is made or a notice given under paragraph (3) the application shall be determined in accordance with regulation 14.

(5) The functions of the tribunal in relation to an application to be determined without an oral hearing may be exercised by a single member of the panel provided for in Schedule 10 to the Rent Act 1977, if he was appointed to that panel by the Lord Chancellor.

Hearings

14.—(1) Subject to regulations 8(3), 9(2) and 10(2), a hearing shall be on the date and at the time and place appointed by the tribunal.

(2) The tribunal shall give notice to the parties of the appointed date, time and place of the hearing.

(3) Subject to paragraph (4), notice under paragraph (2) shall be given not less than 21 days (or such shorter period as the parties may agree) before the appointed date.

(4) In exceptional circumstances the tribunal may, without the agreement of the parties, give less than 21 days notice of the appointed date, time and place of the hearing; but any such notice must be given as soon as possible before the appointed date and the notice must specify what the exceptional circumstances are.

(5) The tribunal may arrange that an application shall be heard together with one or more other applications.

(6) A hearing shall be in public unless, in the particular circumstances of the case, the tribunal decide that a hearing or part of a hearing shall be held in private.

(7) At the hearing—

(a) the tribunal shall determine the procedure (subject to these Regulations) and the order in which the persons appearing before it are to be heard;

(b) a person appearing before the tribunal may do so either in person or by a representative authorised by that person, whether or not that representative is a barrister or a solicitor; and

(c) a person appearing before the tribunal may give evidence on their own behalf, call witnesses, and cross-examine any witnesses called by any other person appearing.

(8) If a party does not appear at a hearing, the tribunal may proceed with the hearing if it is satisfied that notice has been given to that party in accordance with these Regulations.

Postponement and adjournment

15.—(1) Subject to paragraph (2) the tribunal may postpone or adjourn a hearing or pre-trial review either on its own initiative or at the request of a party.

(2) Where a postponement or adjournment has been requested the tribunal shall not postpone or adjourn the hearing except where it considers it is reasonable to do so having regard to—

(a) the grounds for the request;

(b) the time at which the request is made; and

(c) the convenience of the other parties.

(3) The tribunal shall give reasonable notice of any postponed or adjourned hearing to the parties.

Documents

16.—(1) Before the date of the hearing, the tribunal shall take all reasonable steps to ensure that each of the parties is given—

(a) a copy of any document relevant to the proceedings (or sufficient extracts from or particulars of the document) which has been received from any other party (other than a document already in that person's possession or one of which that person has previously been supplied with a copy); and

(b) a copy of any document which embodies the results of any relevant enquiries made by or for the tribunal for the purposes of the proceedings.

(2) At a hearing, if a party has not previously received a relevant document or a copy of, or sufficient extracts from or particulars of, a relevant document, then unless—

(a) that person consents to the continuation of the hearing; or
(b) the tribunal considers that that person has a sufficient opportunity to deal with the matters to which the document relates without an adjournment of the hearing,

the tribunal shall adjourn the hearing for a period which it considers will give that person a sufficient opportunity to deal with those matters.

Inspections

17.—(1) A tribunal may inspect—

(a) the house, premises or area which is the subject of the application; or
(b) any comparable house, premises or area to which its attention is directed.

(2) Subject to paragraph (3), the tribunal shall give the parties an opportunity to attend an inspection.

(3) The making of, and attendance at, an inspection is subject to any necessary consent being obtained.

(4) Where an inspection is to be made in the case of an application which is to be determined under regulation 13, the tribunal shall give notice to the parties.

(5) Where an inspection is to be made before a hearing, the tribunal shall give notice to the parties.

(6) Where an inspection is to be made during or after the close of a hearing, the tribunal shall give notice to the parties at the hearing.

(7) A notice under paragraph (4), (5) or (6) shall—

(a) state the date, time and place of the inspection;
(b) be given not less than 14 days before that date.

(8) Where an inspection is made after the close of a hearing, the tribunal may reopen the hearing on account of any matter arising from the inspection.

(9) The tribunal shall give reasonable notice of the date, time and place of the reopened hearing to the parties.

(10) Any of the requirements for notice in the preceding paragraphs may be dispensed with or relaxed—

(a) with the consent of the parties; or

(b) if the tribunal is satisfied that the parties have received sufficient notice.

Decisions

18.—(1) This regulation applies to a decision on the determination of an application by—

(a) a tribunal; or

(b) a single member, as mentioned in regulation 13(5).

(2) If a hearing was held, the decision may be given orally at the end of the hearing.

(3) A decision shall, in every case, be recorded in a document as soon as possible after the decision has been made.

(4) A decision given or recorded in accordance with paragraph (2) or (3) need not record the reasons for the decision.

(5) Where the document mentioned in paragraph (3) does not record the reasons for the decision, they shall be recorded in a separate document as soon as possible after the decision has been recorded.

(6) A document recording a decision, or the reasons for a decision, shall be signed and dated by an appropriate person.

(7) An appropriate person may, by means of a certificate signed and dated by that person, correct any clerical mistakes in a document or any errors arising in it from an accidental slip or omission.

(8) In this regulation, "appropriate person" means—

(a) where an application was determined by a single member as mentioned in regulation 13(5)—

(i) the single member; or

(ii) in the event of the person's absence or incapacity, another member of the tribunal who was appointed by the Lord Chancellor;

(b) in any other case—

(i) the chairman of the tribunal; or

(ii) in the event of the person's absence or incapacity, another member of the tribunal.

(9) A copy of any document recording a decision, or the reasons for a decision, and a copy of any correction certified under paragraph (7) shall be sent to each party.

Enforcement

19.—Any decision of the tribunal may, with the permission of the county court, be enforced in the same way as orders of such a court.

Permission to appeal

20.—Where a party makes an application to a tribunal for permission to appeal to the Lands Tribunal—

(a) the application shall be made to the tribunal within the period of 21 days starting with the date on which the document which records the reasons for the decision under regulation 18 was sent to that party; and

(b) a copy of the application shall be served by the tribunal on every other party.

Attendance by member of Council on Tribunals

21.—A member of the Council on Tribunals, who is acting in that capacity, may—

(a) attend any hearings held, whether in public or private, in accordance with these Regulations;

(b) attend any inspection for which any necessary consent has been obtained;

(c) be present during, but not take part in, a tribunal's deliberations in respect of an application.

Information required by tribunal

22.—Where a tribunal serves a notice requiring information to be given under paragraph 4 of Schedule 12 to the 2002 Act, the notice shall contain a statement to the effect that any person who fails without reasonable excuse to comply with the notice commits an offence and is liable on summary conviction to a fine not exceeding level 3 on the standard scale.

Notices

23.—(1) Where any notice or other document is required under these Regulations to be given or sent to a person by the tribunal, it shall be sufficient compliance with the requirement if—

(a) it is delivered or sent by pre-paid post to that person at that person's usual or last known address;

(b) it is sent to that person by fax or other means of electronic communication which produces a text of the document;

(c) where that person has appointed an agent or representative to act on that person's behalf—

   (i) it is delivered or sent by pre-paid post to the agent or representative at the address of the agent or representative supplied to the tribunal; or

   (ii) it is sent to the agent or representative by fax or other means of electronic communication which produces a text of the document.

(2) A notice or other document may be sent as mentioned in paragraphs (1)(b) or (c)(ii) only if that person or that person's agent has given consent.

(3) A notice or other document sent as mentioned in paragraphs (1)(b) or (c)(ii) shall be regarded as sent when the text of it is received in legible form.

(4) This paragraph applies where—

    (a) an intended recipient—

        (i) cannot be found after all diligent enquiries have been made;

        (ii) has died and has no personal representative; or

        (iii) is out of the United Kingdom; or

    (b) for any other reason a notice or other document cannot readily be given or sent in accordance with these Regulations.

   (5) Where paragraph (4) applies, the tribunal may—

    (a) dispense with the giving or sending of the notice or other document; or

    (b) may give directions for substituted service in such other form (whether by advertisement in a newspaper or otherwise) or manner as the tribunal think fit.

Allowing further time

24.—(1) In a particular case, the tribunal may extend any period prescribed by these Regulations, or prescribed by a notice given under these Regulations, within which anything is required or authorised to be done.

   (2) A party may make a request to the tribunal to extend any such period but must do so before that period expires.

Revocation and saving

25.—(1) Subject to paragraph (2) the Rent Assessment Committee (England and Wales) (Leasehold Valuation Tribunal) Regulations 1993[173] ("the 1993 Regulations") are hereby revoked in relation to Wales.

   (2) The revocation in paragraph (1) shall not have effect in relation to any application made, or proceedings transferred from a court, to a tribunal before 31st March 2004.

   Signed on behalf of the National Assembly for Wales under section 66(1) of the Government of Wales Act 1998.[174]

John Marek
The Deputy Presiding Officer of the National Assembly
9th March 2004

Regulation 3   Schedule 1

Descriptions of Applications

Enfranchisement and extended leases

   1.—Applications under—

    (a) section 21 of the Leasehold Reform Act 1967[175];

    (b) section 13 of the 1987 Act;

    (c) section 31 of that Act;

    (d) section 24 of the 1993 Act;

    (e) section 25 of that Act;

    (f) section 27 of that Act;

    (g) section 48 of that Act;

(h) section 51 of that Act;
(i) section 88 of that Act;
(j) section 91 of that Act;
(k) section 94 of that Act; and
(l) paragraph 2 of Schedule 14 to that Act.

Service Charges, administration charges and estate charges
2.—Applications under—

(a) section 20ZA of the 1985 Act;[176]
(b) section 27A of that Act;[177]
(c) paragraph 8 of the Schedule to that Act;[178]
(d) section 159 of the 2002 Act;
(e) paragraph 3 of Schedule 11 to that Act; and
(f) paragraph 5 of Schedule 11 to that Act.

Estate management schemes
3.—Applications under Chapter 4 of Part 1 to the 1993 Act.

Regulation 3   Schedule 2

Particulars of Applications

Enfranchisement and extended leases
1.—(1) A copy of any notice served in relation to the enfranchisement.

(2) The name and address of the freeholder and any intermediate landlord.

(3) The name and address of any person having a mortgage or other charge over an interest in the premises the subject of the application held by the freeholder or other landlord.

(4) Where an application is made under section 21(2) of the Leasehold Reform Act 1967,[179] the name and address of the sub-tenant, and a copy of any agreement for the sub-tenancy.

(5) Where an application is made under section 13 of the 1987 Act,[180] the date on which the landlord acquired the property and the terms of acquisition including the sums paid.

Service charges, administration charges and estate charges
2.—(1) Where an application is made under section 27A of the 1985 Act, the name and address of the secretary of any recognised tenants' association.

(2) Where an application is made under paragraph 3 of Schedule 11 to the 2002 Act, a draft of the proposed variation.

(3) A copy of the lease or, where appropriate, a copy of the estate management scheme.

Estate management charges
3.—(1) A copy of any estate management agreement or the proposed estate management scheme.

(2) A statement that the applicant is either—

(a) a natural person;
(b) a representative body within the meaning of section 71(3) of the 1993 Act; or
(c) a relevant authority within the meaning of section 73(5) of that Act.

(3) Where an application is made under section 70 of the 1993 Act, a copy of the notice given by the applicant under section 70(4) of that Act.

(4) Where—

(a) approval is sought for a scheme;

(b) approval is sought to modify the area of an existing scheme; or

(c) approval is sought to vary an existing scheme,

a description of the area of—

(i) the proposed scheme;

(ii) the proposed modification; or

(iii) the proposed variation,

including identification of the area by a map or plan.

(5) Where an application is made under section 70 of the 1993 Act, a copy of any consent given by the National Assembly for Wales under section 72(1) of that Act.

[. . .]

Add new Footnote 164: 1987 (c.31); s. 35(5) amended by s. 163(2) of the Commonhold and Leasehold Reform Act 2002 (c.15) ("the 2002 Act"). The functions of the Secretary of State under s. 35(5) were, so far as exercisable in relation to Wales, transferred to the National Assembly for Wales by art. 2 of and Sch. 1 to the National Assembly for Wales (Transfer of Functions) Order 1999, SI 1999/672. Under s. 177 of the 2002 Act, references to the 1987 Act in SI 1999/672 are to be treated as references to that Act as amended by Pt 2 of the 2002 Act.

Add new Footnote 165: 2002 (c.15); see s. 179(1) for the definition of "the appropriate national authority" as respects Wales.

Add new Footnote 166: See s. 173 of the 2002 Act.

Add new Footnote 167: 1985 (c.70).

Add new Footnote 168: 1993 (c.28).

Add new Footnote 169: Amended by para. 10 of Sch. 2 to the Landlord and Tenant Act 1987.

Add new Footnote 170: SI 2004/683 (W.71).

Add new Footnote 171: 1977 (c.42); to which there are amendments not relevant to these Regulations.

Add new Footnote 172: For who is qualified, see para. 5(3) of Sch. 12 to the 2002 Act.

Add new Footnote 173: SI 1993/2408, as amended by SI 1996/2305, SI 1997/74 and SI 1997/1854.

Add new Footnote 174: 1998 (c.38).

Add new Footnote 175: 1967 (c.88).

Add new Footnote 176: Inserted by s. 151 of the 2002 Act from March 30, 2004 (SI 2004/669 (W.62) (C.25)).

Add new Footnote 177: Inserted by s. 155 of the 2002 Act from March 30, 2004 (SI 2004/669 (W.62) (C.25)).

Add new Footnote 178: Amended by s. 180 of and Sch. 14 to the 2002 Act from March 30, 2004 (SI 2004/669 (W.62) (C.25)).

Add new Footnote 179: Amended by s. 142 and Sch. 22 to the Housing Act 1980.

Add new Footnote 180: Substituted by s. 92(1) and Sch. 6 to the Housing Act 1996 (c.52).

APPENDIX 2V

**Leasehold Reform (Enfranchisement and Extension) (Amendment)
(Wales) Regulations 2004**

(SI 2004/699 (W.74))

1218V   The National Assembly for Wales, in exercise of the powers conferred on the
Secretary of State by section 22(2) of the Leasehold Reform Act 1967[181] and now
vested in the National Assembly for Wales,[182] hereby makes the following
Regulations:

Citation and commencement

    1.—These Regulations may be cited as the Leasehold Reform (Enfranchise-
ment and Extension) (Amendment) (Wales) Regulations 2004 and shall come
into force on the 31st March 2004.

Application

    2.—These Regulations apply only—

    (a) in respect of a leasehold house in Wales;[183]
    (b) to cases where a notice under Part 1 of the Leasehold Reform Act 1967
        (tenant's notice of desire to have or claim to be entitled to acquire the
        freehold or an extended lease) is given on or after the date these
        Regulations come into force.

Amendments

    3.—The Leasehold Reform (Enfranchisement and Extension) Regulations
1967[184] shall be amended as follows—

    (a) in paragraph 2 of Part 1 of the Schedule, after the words "tenancy and"
        insert ", in a case to which paragraph 2A applies,";
    (b) after that paragraph insert—

        "**2A** This paragraph applies where—

        (a) the tenancy in question is a business tenancy; or
        (b) a flat forming part of the house is let to a person who is a
            qualifying tenant for the purposes of Chapter 1 or 2 of Part 1 of
            the Leasehold Reform, Housing and Urban Development Act
            1993,";

    (c) in paragraph 1 of Part 2 of the Schedule after the words "tenancy
        and" insert ", in a case to which paragraph 1A applies,";
    (d) after that paragraph insert—

        "**1A** This paragraph applies where—

    (a) the tenancy in question is a business tenancy; or

    (b) a flat forming part of the house is let to a person who is a qualifying tenant for the purposes of Chapter 1 or 2 of Part 1 of the Leasehold Reform, Housing and Urban Development Act 1993.".

Signed on behalf of the National Assembly for Wales under section 66(1) of the Government of Wales Act 1998.[185]

John Marek
The Deputy Presiding Officer of the National Assembly
9th March 2004

Add new Footnote 181: 1967 (c.88). Section 22(2) was amended by the Transfer of Functions (Lord Chancellor and Secretary of State) Order 1974, SI 1974/1896.

Add new Footnote 182: The powers of the Secretary of State under s. 22(2) of the Leasehold Reform Act 1967 were transferred to the National Assembly for Wales pursuant to art. 2(2) of, and Sch. 1 to, the National Assembly for Wales (Transfer of Functions) Order 1999 (SI 1999/672).

Add new Footnote 183: See s. 2 of the Leasehold Reform Act 1967 (c.88) for the definition of "house".

Add new Footnote 184: SI 1967/1879, to which there are amendments not relevant to these Regulations.

Add new Footnote 185: 1998 (c.38).

APPENDIX 2W

Commonhold and Leasehold Reform Act 2002 (Commencement No.5 and Saving and Transitional Provision) Order 2004

(SI 2004/3056)

1218W The Lord Chancellor, as respects England and Wales, and the First Secretary of State, as respects England, in exercise of the powers conferred on them by section 181 of the Commonhold and Leasehold Reform Act 2002,[186] hereby make the following Order:

Citation and interpretation

1.—(1) This Order may be cited as the Commonhold and Leasehold Reform Act 2002 (Commencement No.5 and Saving and Transitional Provision) Order 2004.

(2) In this Order, unless otherwise stated, references to sections and Schedules are references to sections of, and Schedules to, the Commonhold and Leasehold Reform Act 2002.

[. . .]

Provisions coming into force in England on 28th February 2005

3.—Subject to article 4, the following provisions shall come into force in England on 28th February 2005—

    (a) section 126,

    [. . .]

    (j) section 180, in so far as it relates to the repeals in Schedule 14 of—
        (i) the definition of "the valuation date" in paragraph 1(1) of Schedule 6 to the Leasehold Reform, Housing and Urban Development Act 1993;[187]
        (ii) section 82 of the Housing Act 1996;[188] and
        (iii) in paragraph 18(2) of Schedule 10 to that Act, paragraph (b) and the word "and" before it.

Saving and transitional provision

4.—(1) During the period beginning with 28th February 2005 and ending on the date on which sections 121 to 124 come into force, paragraph 4(2) of Schedule 6 to the Leasehold Reform, Housing and Urban Development Act 1993 shall have effect as if, for "participating tenants", there were substituted "persons who are participating tenants immediately before a binding contract is entered into in pursuance of the initial notice".

[(1A) Section 126 (valuation date) shall not have effect as regards—

    (a) notices given before 28th February 2005 under section 13 of the Leasehold Reform, Housing and Urban Development Act 1993 (notice by qualifying tenants of claim to exercise right);[189] or

(b) applications made before 28th February 2005 under section 26 of that Act (applications where relevant landlord cannot be found).][190]

[...]

Signed by authority of the Lord Chancellor.

David Lammy
Parliamentary Under Secretary of State, Department for Constitutional Affairs
16th November 2004

Signed by authority of the First Secretary of State.

Keith Hill
Minister of State, Office of the Deputy Prime Minister
16th November 2004

Add new Footnote 186: 2002 (c.15). See the definition of "the appropriate authority" in s. 181(4).
Add new Footnote 187: 1993 (c.28).
Add new Footnote 188: 1996 (c.52).
Add new Footnote 189: 1993 (c.28).
Add new Footnote 190: Inserted by Commonhold and Leasehold Reform Act 2002 (Commencement No.5 and Saving and Transitional Provision) (Amendment) (England) Order 2005 (SI 2005/193) art. 2.

APPENDIX 2X

Leasehold Valuation Tribunals (Procedure) (Amendment) (Wales) Regulations 2005

(SI 2005/1356 (W.104))

1218X   The National Assembly for Wales, in exercise of the powers vested in it under section 35(5) of the Landlord and Tenant Act 1987[191] and Schedule 12 to the Commonhold and Leasehold Reform Act 2002,[192] and after consultation with the Council on Tribunals, makes the following Regulations:

Name, commencement and application
1.—(1) These Regulations are called the Leasehold Valuation Tribunals (Procedure) (Amendment) (Wales) Regulations 2005 and shall come into force on 31 May 2005.

(2) These Regulations apply in relation to applications made, or proceedings transferred from a court, to a leasehold valuation tribunal, on or after 31 May 2005, in respect of premises in Wales.

Amendment of the Leasehold Valuation Tribunals (Procedure) (Wales) Regulations 2004
2. The Leasehold Valuation Tribunals (Procedure) (Wales) Regulations 2004[193] shall be amended in accordance with regulations 3 to 8.

Application of Regulations
3. In regulation 1 (name, commencement and application), for paragraph (3), substitute—

"(3) These Regulations apply in relation to any application made, or proceedings transferred from a court, to a leasehold valuation tribunal in respect of premises in Wales on or after—

(a) in the case of an application of the description specified in paragraph 8 of Schedule 1, 31 May 2005;

(b) in any other case, 31 March 2004.".

Particulars of applications
4. In regulation 3—

(a) in paragraph (3), for "paragraph 2", where it first occurs, substitute "any of sub-paragraphs (b) to (f) of paragraph 2"; and

(b) after paragraph (7), insert the following paragraph—

"(7A) Where an application is of the description specified in paragraph 8 of Schedule 1 (determination as to breach of covenant or condition) the particulars and documents listed in paragraph 7 of Schedule 2 shall be included with the application.".

Determination without a hearing

5. In regulation 13(1), for sub-paragraphs (a) to (c), substitute the following sub-paragraphs—

"(a) it has given to both the applicant and the respondent not less than 28 days' notice in writing of its intention to proceed without an oral hearing; and

(b) neither the applicant nor the respondent has made a request to the tribunal to be heard,

but this paragraph is without prejudice to paragraph (3).".

Inspections

6. In regulation 17, for paragraphs (4) to (7), substitute the following paragraphs—

"(4) Where an inspection is to be made, the tribunal shall give notice to the parties.

(5) A notice under paragraph (4) shall—

(a) state the date, time and place of the inspection; and

(b) be given not less than 14 days before that date.".

Descriptions of applications

7. In Schedule 1, after paragraph 7, insert the following paragraph—

"Determination as to breach of covenant or condition

8. Applications under section 168(4) of the 2002 Act.".

Particulars of applications

8. In Schedule 2—

(a) in paragraph 1 (enfranchisement and extended leases), after sub-paragraph (5), insert the following sub-paragraph—

"(6) Except where an application is made under section 24, 25 or 27 of the 1993 Act, a copy of the lease.";

(b) in paragraph 6 (variation of leases), after sub-paragraph (2), add the following sub-paragraph—

"(3) A copy of the lease."; and

(c) after paragraph 6, add the following paragraph—

"Determination of breach of covenant or condition

7.—(1) A statement giving particulars of the alleged breach of covenant or condition.

(2) A copy of the lease concerned.".

Signed on behalf of the National Assembly for Wales under section 66(1) of the Government of Wales Act 1998.[194]

D. Elis-Thomas
The Presiding Officer of the National Assembly
17 May 2005

Add new Footnote 191: 1987 (c.31). Section 35(5) is amended by s. 163(2) of the Commonhold and Leasehold Reform Act 2002 (c.15) ("the 2002 Act"). The functions of the Secretary of State under s. 35(5) were, so far as exercisable in relation to Wales, transferred to the National Assembly for Wales by art. 2 of, and Sch. 1 to, the National Assembly for Wales (Transfer of Functions) Order 1999 (SI 1999/672). Under s.177 of the 2002 Act, references to the 1987 Act in SI 1999/672 are to be treated as references to that Act as amended by Pt 2 of the 2002 Act.
Add new Footnote 192: 2002 (c.15). See s. 179(1) for the definition of "the appropriate national authority" as respects Wales.
Add new Footnote 193: SI 2004/681 (W.69).
Add new Footnote 194: 1998 (c.38).

APPENDIX 2Y

Commonhold and Leasehold Reform Act 2002 (Commencement No.3 and Savings and Transitional Provisions) (Wales) Order 2005

(SI 2005/1353 (W.101))

The National Assembly for Wales, in exercise of the powers conferred upon it **1218Y** by section 181 of the Commonhold and Leasehold Reform Act 2002,[195] hereby makes the following Order:

Name, interpretation and application

1.—(1) The name of this Order is the Commonhold and Leasehold Reform Act 2002 (Commencement No.3 and Saving and Transitional Provision) (Wales) Order 2005.

(2) In this Order, unless otherwise stated, references to sections and Schedules are references to sections of, and Schedules to, the Commonhold and Leasehold Reform Act 2002.

(3) This Order applies to Wales.

Provisions coming into force in Wales on 31 May 2005

2. Subject to article 3, the following provisions shall come into force in Wales on 31 May 2005—

(a) section 126;

(b) section 157, in so far as it relates to paragraph 15 of Schedule 10;

(c) section 164, to the extent that it is not already in force;

(d) section 165;

(e) sections 166 and 167, to the extent that they are not already in force;

(f) sections 168 to 170;

(g) section 171, to the extent that it is not already in force;

(h) in section 172, subsections (1) to (5), except to the extent that they relate to the application to the Crown of sections 21 to 22 of the Landlord and Tenant Act 1985,[196] as substituted or inserted by sections 152 to 154;

(i) section 176 and Schedule 13, to the extent that they are not already in force; and

(j) section 180, in so far as it relates to the repeals in Schedule 14 of—

    (i) the definition of "the valuation date" in paragraph 1(1) of Schedule 6 to the Leasehold Reform, Housing and Urban Development Act 1993;[197]

    (ii) section 82 of the Housing Act 1996;[198] and

    (iii) in paragraph 18(2) of Schedule 10 to that Act, paragraph (b) and the word "and" before it.

Saving and transitional provision

3.—(1) During the period beginning with 31 May 2005 and ending on the date on which sections 121 to 124 come fully into force, paragraph 4(2) of Schedule 6 to the Leasehold Reform, Housing and Urban Development Act 1993 shall have effect as if, for "participating tenants", there were substituted "persons who are participating tenants immediately before a binding contract is entered into in pursuance of the initial notice".

(2) Section 126 shall not have effect as regards—

    (a) notices given before 31 May 2005 under section 13 of the Leasehold Reform, Housing and Urban Development Act 1993; or

    (b) applications made before 31 May 2005 under section 26 of that Act.

(3) Section 168 shall not have effect as regards notices served under section 146(1) of the Law of Property Act 1925[199] before 31 May 2005 in respect of a breach by a tenant of any covenant or condition.

(4) The amendments made by section 170 shall not have effect as regards notices served under section 146(1) of the Law of Property Act 1925 before 31 May 2005.

Signed on behalf of the National Assembly for Wales under section 66(1) of the Government of Wales Act 1998.[200]

D. Elis-Thomas
The Presiding Officer of the National Assembly
17 May 2005

Add new Footnore 195: 2002 (c.15). See the definition of "the appropriate authority" in section 181(4).

Add new Footnote 196: 1985 (c.70). (Sections 21, 21A, 21B and 22 will be substituted or inserted when sections 152 to 154 of the Commonhold and Leasehold Reform Act 2002 come fully into force).

Add new Footnote 197: 1993 (c.28).

Add new Footnote 198: 1996 (c.52).

Add new Footnote 199: 1925 (c.20).

Add new Footnote 200: 1998 (c.38).

INDEX